ISLAM
MUSLIMS
&
NON MUSLIMS

D1665669

TAJ OFFICE,
36, MOHAMMED ALI ROAD
POST BOX No. (3058),
MUMBAI-400003,

ISLAM
MUSLIMS
&
NON MUSLIMS

by
Allama Yusuf Alqarzavi
Abumasood Azhar Nadvi

ADAM PUBLISHERS & DISTRIBUTORS
DELHI-110006 INDIA

ADAM PUBLISHERS & DISTRIBUTERS

Exporters & Importers

1542, Pataudi House, Darya Ganj

New Delhi-110002

Phone (O): 23282550, 23284740

Tele/Fax: 23267510 (R) 95120-2413957

email: apd@bol.net.in

www.adambooks.com

Edition-2004

ISBN: 81-7435-231-7

Printed & bound in India

Published by : S.SAJID ALI

ADAM PUBLISHERS & DISTRIBUTERS

1542, Pataudi House, Darya Ganj

New Delhi-110002

To

The Great Islamic Scholar

and Patriot

Maulana Abul Kalam Azad

CONTENTS

Part I

Part II

Preface

We can do no justice to a faith if we judge it by the faulty practice of its believers and from an opinion regarding the faith on that basis, of course its merits and demerits can only be determined by a fair analysis of the faith itself, by examining its various aspects. It is no fault of the faith if its believers themselves do not follow it and are not found to be committed to its principles and precepts. Likewise, to form a fair opinion regarding Islam it is imperative to judiciously look into its fundamentals and preachings. If Muslims appear not to be fully adhering to the framework of the creed laid down for them, they themselves should be held responsible. To blame Islam for this fact is nothing but injustice and outrage.

There is no room for confusion given all the Islamic canons and precepts are seen fully referring to their context. But regretably, an attempt is made to present some of its commands and preachings by tearing out them from their context and the faults or weaknesses in Muslim's behaviour or conduct are attributed, not to human weakness but to Islam itself.

Islam is a pragmatic religion clearly seen to contain streams of all humane religions and preachings. It never subscribes to look down any prophet or sacred figure; on the contrary it stands guard to the respect, dignity and honour of all. It does not allow contempt of any prophet

(Holy messenger) but is even peculiar to Islamic preachings that a Muslim rejecting or showing contempt to any one of the prophet can no longer remain a Muslim. He must have <u>faith</u> in every prophet. The holy Quran does not mention all the prophets by name but only a few. However, it says in clear terms that all communities have prophets sent to them. The assertion, then, obviously implies that the great souls of various lands who are, for centuries regarded as ideal men might have attained the august place of prophets. Hence it is essential to respect them all.

It is an established historical fact that despite all their moral and practical drawbacks Muslims never showed disregard or blamed the dignified persons of other religions. In contrast the Prophet of Islam Muhammad ﷺ was subjected to countless baseless insinuations and attempts continued to malign and condemn him. This is an evidence, glaring like the day light of the justice and pragmatism of the Islamic precepts.

In the human nature the good and the evil go side by side, as is common with all communities in the world. The same is true with Muslims. Whenever the bonds of Islamic preaching were loosened they fell into practical lapses and omissions. However these omissions have been caused not by Islamic precepts but by distancing away from them. One should clearly bear this in mind in regard to Islam and Muslims that Islamic precepts or preachings and Muslims' behaviour are not one and the same thing. Justice demands that one should understand difference between the two and if any shortcomings are found in the behaviour of Muslims he should attribute them to their person and let Islam be seen in the light of its own principles and precepts. No religion in the world preaches evils and immorality and Islam is even one which most of all urges one for justice, tolerance and equity, morale and humility, love and service of human beings. It values and appreciates others, virtues and worthiness and exhorts its followers to acquire them. It opposes every prejudice, ignorance and vehemently forbids everything bad and unworthy for its followers. How could it tolerate excess on any human being while its own preaching say that all humanity is the family of the God. How can one please the God by misbehaving with a member of His own family and that too when the very Islamic preachings are aimed at constantly seeking God's pleasure?

Besides, it amount to another injustice to tune a blind eye to Muslims virtues and pinpoint their lapses. Can one find any people on earth having nothing but virtue, like angels.

That Muslims in the world today are branded fanatics are accused of intolerance, is the result of ceaseless hostile propaganda. Otherwise a fair study of history would make it obvious that no other people on earth has demonstrated more tolerance, liberalism, equality, freedom of views and expression, and the upholding of the highest values of human rights. Is this not a reality that from Indonesia and Malaysia to Egypt and Turkey non Muslims in the Muslim countries are never subjected to discrimination nor of systematic programmes. As against this Muslim minority in almost every region of the wolrd is illtreated. In communist Russia and Red China they stopped short of nothing in persecuting Muslims. Has any form of barbarism been spared by the Zionists in regard to Palestinian Muslims? From Yugoslavia to Philippines they subjected Muslims of all sorts of tyranny. But all these forces wear the mantle of the torch bearers of progress, liberalism, human rights and equity and benevolence, and Muslims on the other hand, are presented as symbol of intolerance, fanaticism and prejudice.

This book is divided into two parts. The first one contains information on India on how Muslim rulers treated and behaved with non-Muslims here. Everything has been borrowed from 'Maqalate-Shibli' and 'Aurangzeb Alamgeer Par Ek Nazar' by Shibli Noumani, Maqalate Sulaimani by Syed Sulaiman Nadvi, two books by Syed Shahabuddin Abdur Rahman, one by Syed Mohammad Miyan and the well known annual lecture by late Mr. B.N. Pande, former Governor of Orissa on 'Islam and Indian Culture' at Khuda Bakhsh Oriental Public Library. Or it would rather be more correct to say that what follows here is only a systematic compilation of the excerpts from these works.

The second part of the present book is translation from Arabic of the renowned author of Islamic world Yousuf Karzavi's 'Gairul Muslimeen Fil Mujtamail Islami.' In this work the author has endeavoured to show quoting from Quran Hadith and authentic fiqah sources, what is the nature and extent of rights for non-Muslims in an Islamic society, what guarantees are there to fulfil these rights, the responsibilities enjoined upon them, the heights of tolerance taught by Islam, what does its comparison with other people in the world bear out and what does history testifies.

It is prayed that in this age of misconcepts and misgivings may this book succeed, at least to some extent, in letting people see the reality.

★

PART I

by
ALLAMA YUSUF ALQARZAVI

SOME ISLAMIC TERMINOLOGIES

Some Islamic terminologies will be occuring often in the forthcoming pages so it may be appreciated to have a glances at their meaning and the interpretation.

Muslim or Musalman : One who utters Kalma-i-Tauheed, that is, according to the Islamic faith, he believes in the unity and oneness of God and accepts fundamental tenents of Islam.

Momin : One who according to the Islamic faith, sincerely believes in God and does not include anyone else in His person and His attributes.

Kafir : One who refuses to believe in God.

Mushrik : One who includes anyone else in God' person or His attributes.

Murtad : Apostate, one who retreats after having accepted Islam.

Ahle Kitab: Those who believe in any of the revealed scriptures, such as Jews and Christians, who believe in the Torah and the Bible.

Shibhe Ahle Kitab: Those who do not have any of the scriptures mentioned in the Holy Quran, but they are understood to have been the recipients of some scripture at some point of time. Iranian Parsis are taken as such. According to many ulamas, Hindus are also in the same category.

Dhimmi and Moahid : The people of the non -

Muslim territories conquered by Muslim were called Dhimmis, where people entered into a peace agreement without fighting, they were called Moahids. Both sorts of people are called Dhimmis or Ahle-Dhimma. Both have similar rights. But those with whom any agreement was made the terms of the agreement were also to be observed. The rights of the Moahids and Dhimmis can never be altered: they are permanent in their nature.

Jizia: The non-Muslims living in Darul Islam, that is, in Islamic countries, and having the ability to use weapons had to pay a tax in lieu of their exemption from defence responsibilities. Women, Children, the old, the invalid, those who prayed in seclusion and the pauper, were exempted from that tax.

Kheraj: Lands in the conquered areas were left with their actual owners and a levy for that was fixed. The levy for the land remained the same, be it belonged to a non-muslim or bought by a Muslim. But, the Muslims has to pay Zakat for the production of the land in adition to the levy.

Jehad : A war fought for the defence or the security of the Islamic system and only for the sake of God's pleasure without self - aggrandizement or selfish intents.

Harbi : The non-Muslims in a state of war against Muslims.

Darul Islam : The areas under Islamic rule or ruled

over by Muslims.

Darul Harb : The are as ruled over by non-Muslims at war with Muslims.

Darul Amn : The areas under the rule of non-Muslims but where Muslims have religious freedom and the opportunity to live honourably in peace and harmony.

ISLAM, MUSLIMS AND NON-MUSLIMS

With regard to Non-Muslims, there are many misunderstandings rife about Islam and the Muslims. Some of them gained currency due to ignorance or lack of correct information, others have been spread internationally and a good few are the outcome of the mistakes on the part of Muslims themselves. The interesting feature of this is that in India these misunderstandings began to spread after the advent of the Britishers - the so called colonizers, and the process continues with full vigour even now. (Half a century after the departure of foregin rules). Islam is being presented as a religion, narrow-minded and most intolerant, and the Muslims as tyrants, oppressors and people given to hurt the feelings of the others.

Here we are faced with a situation where not only others are ignorant of the Islamic teachings but most of the Muslims themselves have little acquantance with them. The long-drawn history of Muslims,like the history of other peoples and nations, is not lacking in persons we can never be proud of. However, it is also replete with such justice-loving, high-minded, noble persons and their equally noble and magnificent deeds that could be the pride of any nation, which are being hidden from view today. And the bright face of this glorious history of Muslim's is being tarnished and distorted with black and batted lies.

The tragedy of the history of medieval and preceding periods is that it is the history of rules or a detailed documents of their conquests and other achievements, their administration with a plethora of their personal lives, their families and vassals. (It is sadly lacking even in glimpses of the life of the common man in those mighty kingdom whose account fulls volumes). Barring the royal personages and their military commanders, we find little mention of important personalities of that period., engaged in religious, literary and social activities and their extra ordinary achievements in those fields. The result is an incomplete and rather blurred portrait of that period. And it appears, so to say, in that period remote or comparatively recent past, establishment of great empires and petty kingdom, control over their authority and rule, their expansion, and defence against foreign invaders and rebellions inside usurpers, and their own excesses, oppression and tyranny as despotic rulers, together with rolling in luxury and debauchery., were the only feats deemed worthy of rulers. Whereas the facts are contrary to this distorted portrayal. Many great deeds were performed for the benefit of humanity in that period. There was a gradual upward trend in the fields of learning and literature, constructive measures and developments, wisdom and philosophy, science and research and many other fields and great achievements of those thus engaged have come down to us. And where social reform, civilizing and moral improvement, developing and promoting high attributes of human character, preventing oppression and tyranny, redressal of grievances of the oppressed remedying the troubles of the weak and helpless and help and support of the lonely and destitute and other noble deeds are concerned that (so much maligned) period was far superior to the present day state of affairs (with marvellous material progress man in general losing all his fine atributes is fast returning to the state where he is said to have been totally un-civilized.)

In spreading misunderstandings about the Muslims, Christians have been foremost. Toppling the once mighty Roman Empire (and disgraceful repeated defeats of the collective forces of Europe at the hands of Super-general and conqueror Bayazeed Yaldram), and the long drawn serial of latter day crusades were the main reason and source of instigation of this mischief of the part of Christians. Again, when the European powers (after emerging from the darkness of "dark ages"), set out on the compaign of taking over charge of the entire world (Asia, Africa, Americas and Australia) and bringing them under their cultural influence the task of civilizing them (the so-called white-man's burden) was started, the Muslims majority in these Asian and African lands and their own spiteful nature and their nefarious vendetta compelled them to vehemently pursue their propaganda, particularly directed towards the Muslims in these freshly colonized lands. A fairly large band of orientalists was especially groomed and trained for the purpose of distorting the history of Muslims and denigrating them to an extent that a permanent barrier of hatred was created between them and their Non-Muslims countrymen for ever, (so that their new rulers or colonizers making them run at one another's throat, they themselves may rule in an atmosphere of perfect peace. And they did succeed in this attempt of "Divide and Rule".

The well known scholar and an authority as a historian Allamah Syed Sulaiman Nadvi, pointing out this fact in his presidential address at the session of the History Congress, held at Madras (Dec. 1944), says :

"Political game has not spared even the historical information in this country. This is the seed which produces the famous Indian fruit "Phoot" (Dissension and dissent and the name of fruit of the melon family). A good many things could be said about the goodness of Muslim rule in India. But at the close of this chapter of the authority and rule of Muslims in India, came foreigners who had placed their own men incharge of education department, and it was the endeavour of every section of their various groups to impress upon every Indian the superiority of their own government and alongwith that through a stratagem manage to isolate them with feelings of abiding rancour. Among all the disciplines of education, nothing could succeed like history to achieve this end. So they made a regular campaign and kept on writing books on this discipline from the beginning to the end aiming through various routes at their only objective of creating hatred against Muslims in every walk of life.

And now at this stage (about the close of British rule in India) Indians write text books of history for their students. But it is so painful to see that the trend set by the old masters, the colonizers continues. unchanged. Those who are well versed in this branch of knowledge know well enough that history is a raw material (an ore) which can take any form and shape with a little heat of hostile sentiments and a little labour with comenting and joining materials that go into the desired mould. Through their sympathy or orally they can give the ready material any colour in which they are pleased to present it to the simple minded and uninitiated reader. Pulling together a couple of trivialities and cleverly presenting it as a generality or a rule is the easiest trick which passes as a pleasantry. In days gone by history was a subject, an art which aimed at preparing a record of events. And there it ended. Today it is the most ingenious but ignominous art. Through interpretation and reshaping at the speciousness of language, differences in statement of facts, various colours given to them, make statements of true facts totally impossible. Leaving other things alone try to read the history of the recent world wars, stated variously by the warring nations, or try if you like to listen to just one item of news of various broadcasts by different nations or countires, it will bring before you the glaring fact as to what has become of history, what has come to be understood by it, and what purpose it is serving in the hands of most of our present day historians.

It should be carefully kept in mind when writing the history of Muslim rules that they certainly were Muslims but have never been regarded the religious leaders of Islam and the pious souls of the community. If they resorted to some unfair means in their polity, we need not put up an apology for it today or hang our heads in shame. Is there any nation on earth whose monarchs and conquerors came up to the mark in every phase by any standard of judging and there is no blemish on them? No period of history has been free from both types of people, good and bad. Therefore, bringing in religion in the discussion about persons is a grave error. This error has never been committed in the accounts of Hindu and Christian rulers. (Hinduism and Christianity were never made the target of criticism for the misdeeds of those professing these religions). Have England, Scotland, Ireland and Wales not shed one another's blood in the past? But today care is taken to avoid mention of those factors in those conflicts which can enliven the old rivalries and dig out the long burried hatchets. England and France that are allies for the last one century and a half, can never deny that their two lands have witnessed sanguine confrontations and spilling each other's blood freely. However in stating the past unpleasantness great care is exercised to avoid reference to it, and maintaining the atmosphere of friendly relations. Similarly among the Hindu rulers of ancient India whose time was not occupied by military skirmishes against the neighbouring countries and totally unjustifiable conquests and profuse blood shed? Infact most of the time of these Hindu rulers was taken in bloody engagements on the battlefields with their contemporaries. However, the historians have not in the religious wars of Budhists, Jains, Vedic people, the Aryans and Scythians and the aborigines of India demostrated their own partiality through the might of their pens, when it is well known that there were great religious difference among themselves. And this is the right course to adopt. A similar canciliatory attitude is called for also; with regard to the period of the Muslim rule in India.

THE SYSTEM OF THE ISLAMIC RULE

The concept of rule in Islam is viceregency of Allah, which means that the ruler himself is not the sovereign but only responsible for running the machinery of the state according to the divine injunctions. Apparently enough when the created beings, the slaves of Allah, have been called the family of Allah, no excess, tyranny of oppression could be allowed in dealings with them, no matter what their religion and creed. Man as such (a member of the human species) is entitled basically to be meted out justice and equity in dealings with him. Again, the Islamic concept that human beings are all the progeny of Adam implies as a race they belong to the same father and mother. Therefore, any discrimination on the basis of race is simply ruled out. The Prophet himself in his sermon on the occasion of his last pilgrimage, had declared unambiguously : "No Arab has any superiority to a Non-Arab, nor a Non- Arab is superior to an Arab, nor a fair complexioned is superior to his dark complexioned brother." Taqwa (Piety or fear of Allah's displeasure) is the only basis for superiority if any, that means such a person fears the displeasure of Allah and is passing a clean life based on justice and equity.

The basis of the system of governance is mutual consultation and counselling or "Shooraiyat" as it is called in Islamic terminology. Islam does not believe in dynastic rule and never permitted it to any one. That is why during the period of the rightly guided caliphs it never occurred to any one of them to make it limited to his own family. Whenever there was need of a person to handle the affairs of Muslim community, that one among them well known for his piety religiosity and righteousness as well as experience and capability, was elected and entrusted with this sacred and most delicate trust. There was no consideration of any family or tribe in this choice. Again the caliph was not an autocratic ruler. He was only a supervisor and manager of the affairs of the Muslim community, strictly in keeping with the Islamic Shariah but with onerous responsibilities. It is for this reason that it was generally regarded as a crown of thorns and none in that period ever aspired to it. Their Taqwa prompted them to run away from this unique honour of becoming the head of the Islamic state with a back-breaking burden of responsibilities and no powers, privileges and perks. And that must be carried out strictly in accordance with predetermined rules and regulations and on the basis of justice and equity. Therefore history tells us that the rulers of the Islamic State did an existence of great austerity based on piety.

It is the greatest misfortune of mankind that the Islamic order in its pristine purity could not last long enough to dem- onstrate its beneficence to the humanity at large, and the Muslim too disagreed and opted for monarchy like the other nations of the world. However, the mould of their thought and the moral training were more or less reflected in their lives long after the kingdom of Allah in all its glory was lost. Their merits until late in the days of monarchy were the powerful sparks still glowing in the ashes. These merits are totally overlooked but the demerits or infirmities are "Credited" to the account of Islam itself.

Muslim rule in India lasted for a sufficiently long period But it can by no means be termed an Islamic model state, since it was neither established on Islamic ideology and principles nor was there any attempt ever made to run it on Islamic lines. Occasionally an impress of some Islamic ordainments meets. the eye, but this can be regarded much more as a national impress of the Muslims than an Islamic stamp. During this lengthy period of Muslim rule, there have been many benevolent Muslim rulers also. And certainly there were some of those of evil nature and little inclined to beneficence. There have been periods of justice and equity as well as inglorious shows of excesses, incapabilities and corruptions. Some excesses are directly associated with the particular period, with its vexing problem, when military corps and skirmishes were the only mode of establishing monarchies by adventurists. And here Muslims and non-Muslims are seen standing on the same plane. Any venture some adventurist did all he could to get a fooling. And the present day adventurer in the garb of a politician is playing the same dirty game and night before our eyes. (The man at arms had his eyes fixed on the authority and rule only and had little to do with lies, deceit and exploitation of masses which his modern counterpart makes his sole business).

A careful study of the history of Muslim rulers reveals the fact clearly that they oppressed and tyrannized Muslims much more than others, since they feared these rivals much more where rebellion and *coup d'eteat* were concerned. In the wilderness of Karbala merciless murder of Husain, the grandson of the Apostle of Allah, by the military commanders of Yazeed, the repeated attacks on Alvis, their loss of life and property during the Umayyid and Abbasid caliphates, the whole sale massacre of the Umyyids at the hands of the Abbasid caliphs and in India itself the deadly confrontations between Pathans and Mughals, and the repeated long drawn wars between the central government at Delhi and the regional states, are shining examples of this fact— Muslims oppressing and killing Muslims. In India, Muslims have fought and destroyed Muslims much more than Hindus in occassional combats against them, and a Muslim ruler for the expansion and reinforcement of his empire never flinched from or gave any allowance to another Muslim rulers and kingdom in their on-slaughts. The professional men at arms also fully understood this point, that they were enlisted in the army for their personal benefit only and not engage in a holy religious war with other Mujahids against the forces of evil and the order of falsehood. That is why we notice that in the vast armies of the Muslim rulers of India, right from the select commanders to the rank and file, there were Hindus in a dominant majority. And in the armies of Hindu rulers there were Muslim mercenaries in equally over-whelming majority. And the mercenaries of both the communities were pulling their heart and soul in faithfully fighting for their masters who fed them. The worst denigrated Muslim ruler, Aurangzeb had Jai Singh as the chief commander in his fighting forces, and the officers in command of Shivaji's Artillery was a Muslim. The General of Tipu Sultan's army was a Brahmin, Krishna Rao and Muslim mercenaries were fighting on the side of Rajput rulers.

THE ADVENT OF MUSLIMS IN INDIA

The one time governor of Orissa, Mr. B.N. Pandey said in his address at the annual lecture of Khuda Bukhsh Public Library (1985) :

"In 711 A.D. the first Muslim invader, Muhammad Bin Qasim crossed the Arabian Sea to establish the first Muslim empire in Sind, after defeating Rajah Dahar. When the Arab Commander got to Alaur, the local people put up a strong resistance for several months. Then they came to terms and signed a peace treaty on two conditions: Fristly that no citizen shall be put to the sword and secondly that there should be no meddling with their places of worship. Muhammad Bin Qasim gave assent to these requests saying that the places of worship of the Hindus shall receive the same respect, regard and immunity as those of the Jews,

Christian and Gnebres has enjoyed."

Arab Hind Ta'ulluqat, Syed Sulaiman Nadvi, Page 194).

With regard to the invasion of Sind there are two things worth taking careful note of. Firstly, the oppresion and tyranny of the indiginous rulers became the main cause of the triumph of the Arab invaders. Secondly, immediately on the cessation of hostilities after heavy losses and peace treaty was announced, with regard to Civil administration, a polity based on enlightenment was immediately adopted, contrary to this barbaric incidents of the European history of that period, the so called 'dark ages'.

A few examples of the ordainments enforced by Muhammad Bin Qasim are given below :

He ordered that every one in that city should be given silver worth 12 dirhams since they have suffered heavy losses. To create a feeling of security among the populace, he appointed the local outstanding person for the realization of the revenues of the state.

— Ishwari Prasad, Medieval History of India, Page 59

Muhammad Bin Qasim maintained the social status of Brahmins and their honour dignity and prestige. He issued orders in this behalf. He also provided protection to them against any opposition and violence to which they were exposed. (It must have been even in that distant past period due to their time-honoured Brahmanism which is another name for suppression extortion and exploitation of the non-Brahmins and lower castes as also aborigines who must have thanked their stars for the new-comers as deliverers, but must have also tried to get square with their Brahmin "benefactors"). Every Brahmin was honoured with some important dignified job.

Muhammad Bin Qasim's uncle and his immediate superior Hajjaj, the governor of Iraq, wrote to him in a letter : "Now that the Hindus have surrendered to the conquerors and are willing to pay "Khiraj" to the Caliph at Damascus, no other demands can be made on them. They have come under our protection now, and we cannot in any way lay hands on their lives or properties. They should be perfectly free to worship their deities. No one can be prevented from following his religion. They can live in their homes as they are pleased. (There should be no meddling with the ways of living of the people. It would be an encroachment on their fundamental rights).

Muhammad Bin Qasim directed their leaders and other oustanding citizens together with Brahmins that they could build their temples if they liked, should try to be on friendly terms with the Muslims and get busy with the improvement of their condition fearlessly. He also directed them to be kind to Brahmins. He encouraged and helped them in keeping to their ancient heritage of customs and manners, as also endowed the Brahmins with free grants of lands and gifts as of old.

Mahmud Ghaznawi's fundamental objective was to establish one empire for himself from Punbjab to the river Euphrates, and his repeatedly invading India was with the sole purpose of provision of means to achieve that bigger end. He aimed even at making the caliph of the Muslim world subservient to this own super plans. That is why he invaded the centres of wealth in India, one after the other but never seriously gave thought to rule over this country. The interesting fact is that his army has a large number of Indian soldiers brought here in confrontation with their own countrymen. Undoubtedly Ghaznavi has a favourable opinion of the military skill of Hindus, and they in their turn has no hesitation in serving a foreign invader on their own soil. Mehmud's son, Masood, in his war against his brother, utilised the services of Servinda Rao and to punish the governor of Indian province. Niyaltagin, he had sent Jai Sen's son Tilak. Again, he enlisted the services of Hindus and recruited a large army for the combat against the Suljuqi Turks, and his successor sent the kotwal (the officer responsible for the internal security and peace) of Ghazni itself to bring back a reconciled Hindu general who had left due to some differences with the authorities.

The invasions of Mahmud Ghaznavi and Qutbuddin Aibak can be regarded as triumphant marches, made easy for them by the mutual quarrels of Rajput rulers of northern India. In less than the quarter of a century the entire northern India had fallen into the hands of the conquerors from the north west. But the establishment of a Muslim state here meant nothing more than Muslim military men and administrators replacing the Hindu rulers and their corrupt administration.

Sir Wessly haig, writes in Cambridge History of India, vol. III, P. 89 :

The eloquence of the early Muslim histrorians lavished with regard to such matter as crushing rebellions, arson of forts, cities and villages and laying waste the entire regions, would have gone to support the view that most of the early Muslim invasions of India were aimed at propagaion of Islam and elimination of idol worship. But the facts totally belie this view. From Mahmud to the latter day Muslim invaders, always accepted the subservience of the Hindu rajahs and landlords whose hereditary estates were left in their possession........
.......moreover the Muslim rulers won over the Hindu masses and gained their confidence and support and the administrative machinery at the lower level was entrusted to their care. The land revenue and the financial system remained practically in the hands of Hindus. Undoubtedly rebellion was crushed mercilessly and at least there were excesses also in these corrective measures, but religion was not the factor responsible for them. There is no reason to believe that a Hindu cultivator under a Muslim land lord was any the worse than his Hindu counterpart under a Hindu zamindar.

PROPAGATION OF ISLAM

Allamah Syed Sulaiman Nadvi writes in his papers "Propagation of Islam in India :"

"Of all the religions in the world Islam is the only faith that gave to the world the philosophy that religion is another name for Belief. And Belief cannot be created in any body with the edge of a sword or the point of a spear."

There is no compulsion in religion.

(Q. II : 256)

The Prophet is warned :

Will thou then compel mankind, against their will to believe -   Al Quran X : p. 99.

Allah said it is not the duty of the Prophet to compel people to believe but call to faith and taking the message to them.

Thou art not one to manage (men's) affairs.

-Al Quran LXXXVIII : p. 22

Again,

Thy duty is to convey the message.   (Q. III : P. 20)

The Quran also pointed out how the Divine Faith is to be propagated :

Invite (all) to the way of the Lord with wisdom and beautiful preaching and argue with them in ways that are best most gracious.   (Q.XVI : 125).

If it is true that Islam spread by the sword, what answer can be given to Carlyle's query : "which sword did make these first swordsmen Muslims?" On this principle what ought to have been the shape of things is this that Islam would have been conspicuous by its total absence where its swordsmen neve found access. Where as it is a well known fact that the Muslims never unsheathed their swords in Abyssinia, for their one time good turn in offering the earliest Muslim migrants from Makkah in a state of persecution at the hands of Pagans. However, half its population comprises Muslims. In those parts of Africa which Muslim mujahids never visited, how are Muslims in such large number present there? Muslim armies never invaded China. How forty million Muslim population of China is to be accounted for. The Malayan peninsula and its neighbouring islands have always remained immune from the invasion of Muslims. Yet there are four million Muslims there. Where did they come from is any body's guess. Thailand, Phillipines and other regions of Far East whose soil the feet of Muslim soldiers never touched, how did Islam manage to set foot there? The Turks and Tartars had themselves attacked and massacred Muslims in their home lands, whose swords converted them to Islam?

The patent fact is that Islam's advancement and progress in India was due to the same factors that were responsible for the other religions for which their preachers gave a call. And it is going on now and shall continue in future also under the same principle of peaceful propagation.

The first and the oldest reason for propagatoin of Islam in India was the business relationship of Arab and Hindu leaders. These relations had existed between the Arabs and the coastal population of western India from ancient times. They have existed long before the advent of Islam in Arabia. However, with the organization of Arabs under the influence of Islam, these relations became further strengthened. And at this stage they did not only bring the merchandise from the European countries and their own products and manufactures to India, but began to take with them their most valuable gift, received through their Prophet, Muhammad Sal'am. And from here (India) they did not take back to their own country and thence to Europe, not only spices, perfumes, swords and fine muslins and prints, but a number of new converts to their faith also with them. Malabar, Sind, Gujrat, Kuchh, Kokan, Coastal Bengal and the Islands of India came to regard them as angels of mercy.

The Moplas and Nawayats of Malabar are the progeny of these early Arab traders who used to visit for trade and commerce with the coastal regions of India in the beginning, and they are the first ever preacher of Islam in India.

Sind is the next route of the entry of Islam in India. It has been a tributary of Iran since long and men from Jats and Medlys were the soldiers of their armies. And when Iran fell into the hand's of Muslim's as a legacy of the former Persian Empire, its realtions with Sind also got transferred to them. And from that time upto the invasion of Muhammad Bin Qasim (712 A.D.), relations of peace and its breach had existed between the Muslim rulers of Iraq and the lords of Sind in quick succession. The expansion of Muhammad Bin Qasim's conquests, from Baluchistan and Karachi to Multan, came to an end soon enough. For, it did not last even a hundred years. But the religious conquests of Islam continued all the same.

The appearance of Islam in Arab and the down fall of Budhism in India were contemporary events. However, even on its last legs it did manifest its activities for a sufficiently long time. The Muslim Arabs arriving in Malabar, Ceylon, Sind, Gujrat and Kokan etc., were not confronted by the Hindus belonging to the vedic religion but had to face the follower of Budhism and Jainism. At this time Budhism dominated the vast regions extending from Turkestan to Kabul and from Punjab and Kashmir to Sind and Gujrat and neighbouring regions were under the influence of Jainism. And in Malabar and neighbouring areas instead of the followers of vedic religion, the aborigines of India. Eliot's History of India, Vol. I, also bears testimony to this fact.

The third well know avenue of the advent of Islam into India is that the Khaibar Pass. By this route it gained entry four hundred years after its birth.......................But before that different corners of India had been a glow with the light of Islam, and it had come to be counted as one of the religions of this country, India. However meagre the number of Muslims but they had spread from the river Indus to Qannauj, Multan and Kashmir.

-Maqalat-e-Sulaiman, Part-I

Many misunderstandings have been spread in connection with the propagation of Islam in India. And the worst of them is that Islam was propagated in India through violence and compulsion under the shade of the Muslim monarch's swords. When the fact is that long before the establishment of the Muslim empires in India, the Arab traders had spread Islam in South India. Propagation of Islam in India succeded due to its intrinsic worth and unparalleled merits. The Muslim monarchs never evinced any interest in its propagation or its exaltation. Rather, the fact is that the regions where Muslim monarchs rules for centuries and even in their capitals the proportion of Muslim population is far below that of the regions where they never ruled, if at all for a very brief period. Delhi, Uttar Pradesh, Bihar and Hyderabad present its explicit examples, where after centuries of Muslim rule, Muslim population could not go beyond 15% whereas in such distant regions as Kerala, Bengal and Assaam the ratio is much higher.

Truth to tell, this winning over the heart of non-Muslims was due to the outstanding attributes of Islam like its all embracing nature, unity of Allah in the most unadulterated form, intellectual concept of life social equality and collective unanimity.

The majority of the Indian population was so sick of the divisions due to caste system and social discrimination on that basis that in Islam they found redressal of all their grievances and an honourable life with perfect immunity to hazards of life and property. Naturally they embraced Islam in large numbers, and Islam began to spread as a powerful movemnet in such a manner that it became a challenge to the local customs and manners and their pattern of life in general. And as a reaction many reformation movements began to emerge from the Hindu society.

The Muslim Ulama (those learned in the religious law) presented Islamic teachings to the people and won the hearts of many with their high moral behaviour and ideal character.

Sufis too have played a great role in the propagation of Islam in India. In Madura and Trichanapally Baba Nath-Doly (D. 1039 A.D.) was responsible for spreading Islam. He was a Turkish prince, who abdicating his throne and renouncing the world had taken to asceticism and got to Trichanapally after travelling through Hijaz, Iran and northern India and so much influenced the local population with his devotion and a life of abstinence, worship and high morality that many Hindus there embraced Islam at his hands. He lies burried in Trichanapally. His successor, Syed Ibrahim Shaheed (d. 564 A.H. / 1168 A.D.) also ruled over this region for twelve years. His mausoleum is in Wadi. Another disciple and successor in the religious hierarchy Baba Fakhruddin (564 A.H. - 1168 A.D.) converted the rajah of Pelukonda to Islam. In Madura, Islam was propagated by Baba Ali Badshah, who had come from Baghdad with the party of Baba Raihan to Bharoch, and had converted the son of the local rajah to Islam. Nuruddin Sataqar propagated Islam among the Kambab, Karib and Kharwa Communities of Gujrat, and converted them all to Islam who have taken to Ismaili cult. In 1304 A.D., among the Arab preachers, one gained particular renown a certain Peer Mahabeer Khandayat. He came down to Bijapur and converted the local cultivators to Islam. In the fourteenth century Khowajah Gesu Daraz propagated Islam among the Hindus of Poona and Belgaum. In Kokan, a religious celebrity of the progeny of Syed Abdul Qadir Jilani, Baba Ajab propagated Islam and got buried in Dhanun. In the districts of Dahwar Hashim Peer Gujrati became the means of propagation of Islam. In Satara a fresh convert to Islam, Peer Shamboo Appa Koshi converted the local population to Islam. In the twelfh century a reverted person Syed Ahmad Sultan Safi Sarwar, better known as Lakhi Data (D. 577 A.H. / 1181 A.D.) came to Shahkot, adjacent to Multan and settled there. Both Hindus and Muslims became devotee to him. His followers go by the name of Sultani and are found in fairly large numbers in Punjab, particularly in Jullundhur. In Rajasthan many Hindus embraced Islam through the efforts of Khawajah Moinuddin Chishti. We are told that on his way from Delhi to Ajmer alone he had converted seven hundred Hindus to Islam. Western Punjab was blessed with Islam due to the efforts of Khawajah Bahauddin Zakaria Multani and Baba Fareeduddin Ganjshakar (D. 664 A.H. / 1265 A.D.). In "Jawahir Faridi" it has been said that Baba

Ganjshakar, through his education and preaching brought to the Fold of Islam in eleven different communities of Punjab. Baba Bin Ali Qalandar (D. 724 A.H.) converted three hundred Rajputs in Punjab to Islam. In Kashmir, Shah Mirza Balbul Shah, Shah Syed Ali Hamdani (D. 1384 A.D.) and Mir Shamsuddin Iraqi, were the promoters of the cause of Islam. In Bihar, a reverted person of the Firdausiah cult remained engaged in the preaching and propagation of Islam. In the fifteenth century when Jat Mal, the son of Rajeh Kans of Bengal embraced Islam, through his influence a large number of Hindus entered the fold of Islam.

The successor designate of Nizamuddin, Shaikh Sirajuddin (D. 1357 A.D.) and his successor Ala-ul-Haq (D. 1398 A.D.) stayed in Bengal and long with the unity of Allah and prophethood, brought to the force, Islamic equality, influenced by which the low caste Hindus who were looked down upon with contempt in their own community entered the fold of Islam in hordes. In Sylhet, the disciple of Shaikh Shahabuddin Suharwardi and a brother disciple of Zakarai Multani, Shaikh Jalaluddin Tabrezi (D. 1225 A.D.) propagated Islam. His tomb can be seen in Sylhet.

Muslim Ulama and writers did their best to understand the belief and customs and manners of the indigenous people very sympathetically, and instructed Muslims to respect the Hindu religious leaders in the same way as other religious leaders were respected by them. According to Mirza Mazhar Jan Janan (D. 1195 A.D.), Hindu idol worship is different from the pre-

Islamic idol-worship of the Arabs. He (Mirza) as a staunch believer in Islam regarded the Islamic Shariah as the only way of life to be followed discarding all other obsolete ones as useless. But he has fully instructed his followers to respect the Hindu avatars (god-incarnate) saying that to associate unbelief with those dead and gone without sanctions of the Shariah would not be permissible. In 'Muqamat Mazhari' it has been said that one day dream was related to Mirza Sahib that Ramchandraji was standing by a fire burning in wilderness and Krishnji was in the fire itself. Mirza Sahib interpreted it saying that the fire was the conflagration of love. Krishan's life was one of love, therefore he appeared amid the flames; while Ramchandraji who was a man given to abstinence and sacrifice in the dream appeared standing off. Then he quoted the verse from the Quran.

AND THERE NEVER WAS A PEOPLE WITHOUT A WARNER, HAVING LIVED AMONGST THEM (in the past) (Q. XXXV : 24).

It makes it manifest that there must have been warners and givers of glad-tidings to the Hindus as well. And it is just possible Ramchandraji and Krishna were prophets. Ramchandra is believed to have been sent to this world in the early period when men used to be long-lived and had greater physical strength. Therefore he trained people in keeping with the system of suluk. Krishnji came to the world when longivity had departed and weakness had crept into the human flesh. Therefore, he trained them in his time in the manner of Jazb. And his music and flute, (even dance with Gopis the so-called "Rasleela") are proof of his own Jazb.

Mirza Sahib looks Ved as a revealed book and regarded Hindus as the people of the Book.

Amir Khusro also acknowledged the Hindu concept of the unity of Allah. He has said that Hindus do not believe in our faith but many of their Beliefs are similar to ours. They acknowledge unity of Allah, His entity and Precedence. The providence, creation at will, Independence of acion and His knowledge of part and whole. In this connection Amir Khusro has compared Hinduism with other religions barring Islam, and has proved its superiority to them all giving reasons for it that the dualists are polytheists, but Hindus believing in the unity of Allah are free from it. The Christians take the apostle of Allah, 'Isa ibn Maryam (Jesus son of Mary) as the son of God, but the Hindus are free from such nonsense. The religious sect believing in Allah having a physical existence with a material body like ours are also inferior to Hindus who do not believe in His having a body as an abiding feature[1] The people worshipping stars have seven gods, but the Hindus believe in nothing like that. The sect Mushabbih or Analogist likens Him to a possibility. The Hindus, however, do not believe in any such thing. The Parsis believe in Gods of Light and Darkness. But the Hindus are free from such dualism. They certainly worship stones, animals, the sun and the trees. But there is perfect

----

1.(but His incarnation in the form of an avatar is a sad commentary on it. Tr.).

sincerity in their worship of these objects, since they regard them as the creation of one creator, obedience to whom they do not deny. They worship them because their forefathers before them worshipped these things.

Amir Khusro is very much impressed by the feelings of Hindu women and their faithfulness. He says that Hindu can lay down his life with sword and fire to prove his faithfulness and a Hindu woman can jump into the flames of her husband's funeral pyre. A Hindu male can cheerfully lay down his life for his beloved idol and his master. He goes on further to say.

"Oye who haunt the Hindu for his idol worship.

Learn also the sinceritry and devotion from him".

Again he has praised every thing associated with Hinduism and Hindustan. He has instructed his co-religionists (Muslims) to love and have due regard for Hindustan. In praising the Hindi language, Hindustani (unsewn) dressers, Hindustani flowers, dry fruits, birds and the beauty of Hindu women, his pen appears to have gone out of his control (dancing with ecstasy). For thus winning the hearts of Hindus he used Hindi language for his poetic art, thus leaving a permanent impress on the hearts of Hindus, of his love for them Pandit Jawahar Lal Nehru writes in his "Discovery of India" : Amir Khusro has wirtten on different subjects, particularly he has praised the things of India in which India excels. The Indian religion, philosophy, logic, Sanskrit language, Grammer, Music, Mathematics, Science and mango fruit caught his imagination, but he gained fame mostly due to his songs which has written in simple, easily intelligible language. Pandit Nehru also goes on to say that he never met an example any where that songs wirtten six hundred years earlier might still be going strong as ever and sung with relish without the slightest change in the melodious old diction.

Following the example of Amir Khusro, many other Muslim poets utilised their poetic skill in Hindi and Sanskrit languages. The list of such names is long enough. However, the selected few are given here : Daood, Qittin, Malik Mohammad Jaisi, Sheikh Nabi, Qasim Shah, Noor Muhammed, Taj, Jamal Abdur Raheem Khankhana, Qadir, Mubarak, Alam, Shaikh Shah Muhammad, Nizamuddin, Madhunayak, Syed Rahmatullah, Mir Abdul Jeleel Balgrami, Ghulam Nabi, Syed Barkatullah, Muhammad Arif, Shah Kazim and others.

And during the recent past aslo, Muslim writers have been giving proof of their open mindedness and singing songs of love and unity with the country of their birth. A sufi and a revered person among writers, Khowajah Hasan Nizami of late lamented memory paid homage to Krishnji by writing Krishna Diti. And the great Urdu philosopher poet, Allamah Iqbal, has mentioned Ramchandraji in such beautiful words and in such a grand manner which is perhaps unparalleled in the entire collection of Hindi poetry also :

The wine of Reality fills the cup of Hindustan.

All The philosopher of the west are subdued to Ramchandraji.

The far reaching effect of the thought of Hindutsan is that it is far higher than the skies.

In this country there have been thousands of men with angelic nature.

Whose names have raised Hindustan in the world esteem.

Hindustan is proud of the mere existence of Ram.

Those with far sight regard him as the leader of Hindustan,. Themarvel of this source light (of guidance) is this,

That the evenings of Hindustan are brighter than the mornings elsewhere in the world.

Given to swordsmanship and unique in valour,:

He was also unique in the matter of purity and passionate love.

The great Sufis (mystics) themselves wrote distiches, (dohas), in Hindi, Shaikh Sharfuddin Yehya Maneri, Shaikh Abdul Haq Radaulvi, Shaikh Abdul Quddus Gangohi are famous for their distiches. The colour of Bhajan (Hindu devotional song) was given to Qawwali (Muslim devotional song), to win the hearts of the Hindus. The mystics with their softspokenness, love and affection, gentleness and civility of behaviour, broad mindedness in dealings, breadth of vision and human attitude continuosly tried to draw non-Muslims towards themselves. Shaikh Nizamuddin Auliya freely met and talked to Hindu yogis and listened to them attentively.

According to Farid-ul-Fareed once a Yogi came to Baba Fariduddin Ganj Shakar at Ajodhan and fairplay. They were constantly at pains to make Hindustan a great and magnificent state. And giving it the concept of unity in disparity and diversity they brought together the tiny states of varying sizes, spread all over the country into a strong Union of states, made India a great and powerful country, so much so that the Tortaric deluge from central Asia in its full fury all over Asia, lured not cast an evil eye on it. The fear of the might of Muslim monarchs here compelled them to keep their hands off India.

Along with that military geniues and skills, the Muslim monarchs were also gifted with a high human attitude and excellent morality. They had been very carefully taught the lesson that the entire humanity is the family of Allah and so its service can brook of no discrimination. The Islamic teachings of public service and dispensation of justice they had to keep in view very carefully. The Ulama and mystics of India also kept instructing them in this behalf. So love of justice and its fair dispensation continued to be the distinctive mark of Muslim monarchs of India. Syed Shahabuddin Abdur Rehman writes in his book, "A look at the relationship between the Muslim monarchs; Ulama and other revered Personages", that according to the statement of Fakhr-e-Mudabbir, Qutbuddin Aibak lived to emulate Abu Bakr in generosity and Umar in justice and fairplay (Allah be pleased with both of them). In Fawaidus-Salikin of Bakhtiyar Kaki (Peace be on him). we find: Ailtamash (Altutmish) had it proclaimed in his kingdom that whoever was faced with hunger should be brought to him. And he never returned any of them empty-handed. He instructed them on oath that whenever they were again faced with the same Ganj Shakar at Ajodhan and Shaikh Nizamuddin Auliya asked him, which way of life you have chosen for yourself? He said in reply, "our religious sources of knowledge tell us that there are two trends of thought and action in human nature. One of them is the higher state (Alam Alvi) and the other is a lower of baser (Alam Sifli). From the head down to the navel it is the superior and nobler realm, and from the navel to the feet it is the lower or the baser realm.

In the upper superior realm there are truth, clearliness, high morality and fairness of dealings. And in the lower region there are careful watch, purity and righteousness. On learning this from him Shaikh Nizamuddin Auliya said, "What you said I liked it very much."

Similarly, another Yogi came to Fariduddin Ganj Shakar's monastery and talked about the birth of children to which Nizamuddin Auliya listened with live interest, and said to him, "I have carefully stored in my memory whatever you have said. Listen also attentively to what I am going to say."[1]

---

1 For great detail please see "A look at the relationship between the Muslim monarchs, Ulamas and Mashaekh, by late Syed Sabahuddin Abdur Rahman.

JUSTICE LOVING MONARCHS

In establishing empires in this country it was never the aim of Muslims Monarchs to plunder the wealth of this country, India like Britishers, and after thus robbing us take it to their own lands. Coming to India they meant to stay here permanently and make it their home land. They never allowed the wealth of this country to go anywhere outside. They did everything in their power to make this country a land of peace and plenty and tried to run the state on the basis of hardship or faced oppression, they should rush to him and pulling the chain hanging outside inform him of their need so that he may be able to meet it or dispense justice that was needed. It was beyond his powers to meet the situation created by their complaints on Doomsday. About Ghayasuddin Balban Maulana Ziyauddin Barni has written: "In the matter of dispensation of justice he never cared who was the oppressor and what his position. His brother's sons and the closely associated courtiers being no exception. He could not rest contented and satisfied until he had done justice to the oppressed and punished the guilty. Since he never allowed his own relationship with the oppressor to stand between the parties concerned, his closest relaions, nobles at the court, petty rulers under him and the stalwarts in the public affairs were well-acquainted with this attribute of his meeting out justice to the oppressed. Even the Hindus of this period have spoken very highly of him in this regard. An engraved pillar of 1337 Bikrami/1280 A.D. in Sanskrit has been discovered at Palam which speaks of the prosperity in the realm of Balban. "In his very vast and welfare state right from Ghaur to Ghaznah and from Dirawar to Rameshwaram every where peace and prosperity reigns supureme. His armies have managed to maintain perfect peace which his people enjoy everywhere. The Sultan takes such good care of his people that (God) Vishnu, finding himself free from the management of the affairs of the world has gone to sleep soundly in the sea of milk." Amir Khusro writes in his *Khazain-e- Futuh* about Alauddin Khilji that he has established an order of justice and equity like that of Umar, the second rightly guided caliph and in public affairs he is the true picture of Al-Mustamar billah and al Mustasam (the two well-known caliphs of Abbasid dynasty). About Muhammad bin Tughlaq, the historians of the days of Muslim monarchs of Delhi and the Mughal period say that in dispensation of justice he did not care even about the Ulama and the religious elders. If they were found guilty, he would punish them unhesitatingly. In *Masalik-ul-Absar* it has been recorded for us that the Sultan used to hold durbar-e-aam on Saturdays every week, and on the occasion of its manguration an announcer to make a loud proclamation that the oppressed and tyrannized should come forward with their complaints and the needy and the indigent should put up their needs. Whoever has any complaint or is needy, should come forward with it. At this call the needy and the complainants came in view of the royal seat without any restraint or hesitation on their own part and stated the state of their own affairs, without fear. None dare interrupt a complainant during its presentation or statement at the court. In both the *Tarikh-e-Mubarak Shahi* and Mulla Abdul Qadir Badayuni's *Muntakhab*

Tawarikh it has been stated that the king had appointed four Muftis in his own palace itself. Whenever a complainant came to call at the Royal Palace, the Sultan after listening to him in their presence, consulted them and they would have been previously warned that in case of making any mistake, any innocent person suffering death penalty due to their carelessness, his blood would go to their account in the life Hereafter. So the Muftis were very careful in the judgement of cases. Even the present days historians acknowledge this fact that the reign of Firoz Shah was one of justice to be meted out to him. There was perfect peace in the country. There was plenty of peace and both the classes and the masses were satisfied. The general public was contented and also well off.

The tradition of the dispensation of justice established by the monarchs at Delhi, the Mughals following in their foot steps maintained it still more gloriously. Babar has himself written in his *Tuzak* that while his army was passing through Bhirah, he came to know that his soldiers laying hands on them had roughly treated the local population. The culprits were at once arrested. Some of them were put to the sword and others met the ignominy of a chopped off nose and publicising of the same. Abul Fazal says that Akbar used to devote 1 1/2 Pahr every day to listen to complaints and make out justice to the aggrieved. Jahangir was still more strict in this matter. He listened to the complaints of the common people for two hours every day. He had a chain hung with one end in his palace and the other outside, so that any one could directly reach him and seek justice. Even on journeys he would stop for three hours and hold a provisional court to listen to the complaints of the people around and to punish the guilty. Even sickness did not prevent him from this daily routine. He has written in his *Tuzk*: "For looking into the affairs of the servants of Allah I have to keep awake for some time and undergo trouble and inconvenience so that all of them may be consoled and put at ease. He had some how prepared himself to pass death sentence on Noor Jehan, his beloved queen, meaning life itself to him (Jahangir) for the murder of a washerman. Maulana Shibli Nomani has versified the event in beautiful and moving language, bringing out the high sense of duty to justice as a king, of much greater value to him than his profound love for the "Light of the World" (Noor Jehan).

It was customary with the Mughal kings that they listened to the complaints of the common people where the lowest of the low in society could approach them for the redressal of his grievances. Whoever wanted, presenting himself at Darbar-e-Aam could put up his case for decision. The officials at the court put it up to the king himself, who gave an attentive hearing to a written complaint and then questioned the complainant, giving his decision at the end (of all hearings with evidences) to be put into effect through proper agencies. Even if the guilty person was some office bearer or a member of the royal family, there was never any hesitation in bringing him to the scaffold. Shah Jahan sentenced Hafiz Muhammad Naseer, (All powerful) Nazim (governor) of Gujrat, to life imprisonment because it was found that his treatment of the local traders was one of cruelty. Similarly, he once sacked Fidai Khan, Nazim of Bengal on a complaint of irregularity filed by the public. The worst critics of Aurangzeb cannot accuse him of injustice or even any slackness in dispensation of justice. He had written to Shah Jahan in a letter after his dethronement and divestment of all his powers: "Allah confers powers and authority on only those who have the capability to improve the condition of the subjects and their protection from all sorts of harm. Supervision means keeping an eye on their affairs and providing perfect securtiy to them and not self-indulgence and debauchery.

And it was the result of this love of justice that the kings who were religious-minded and rather strict in its practice, in spite of raising the question of imposing jizyah and permission of making new temples, never compelled the non-Muslims of the sub-continent to embrace Islam. Certainly, they themselves were the protectors of the faith and had to keep an eye on its well-being and promotion of its cause. They tried also to make the Muslims conform to the Islamic way of life and live upto the divine injuctions, carefully keeping out of the way of prohibitions, but never interfered with the religious beliefs of their non-Muslim subjects, nor did they ever play havoc with their social pattern of life by confusing and confounding it. Akbar did try to put a stop to Sati or self-immolation of the Hindu widow on the husband's funeral pyre. It was resorted to on the basis of human consideration alone. He wanted to prevent the inhuman treatment meted out to the minor or very young widows, took some practical steps to stop child marriage, but never brought pressure to bear on compliance with any of these issues; his own wishes and feelings of sympathy notwithstanding. Some rulers are accused of compulsive preaching for change of creed, but careful examination of these cases of so-called compulsion have proved false and baseless. Hindu historians write that U.P. remained under Muslim rule for six hundred years, but the proportion of Muslims in its population is only fourteen per cent. And this is proof of the fact that Hindu religion remained immune from compulsive forces and that propagation of Islam under pressure is a myth. Backwardness was not thrust on Hindus under multi-pronged plans of degradation. All the monarchs of various dynasties had fully understood that their own political well-being depended largely on a policy of non-interference in the people's religious and social systems; without this much of tolerance, their kingdoms would be shaky and likely to be toppled over any moment. The instruction of public service and love of justice imparted by the mystics and their own excellence tolerant behaviour, with the non-Muslims was a source of strength to the Sultan (Monarchs). It must be carefully kept in mind that the kings that have come for mention in the foregoing statements were the good rulers of the days of Muslim rule at its zenith in India. If they had not been gifted with these attributes, in this land of valiant Rajputs who could readily lay down their lives for any cause cherished by them, noble or ignoble, would have made it impossible for them and their co-religionists to get an easy foothold on their soil. They could easily made it ruddy with their own and their enemy's blood. So it will have to be acknowledged that during the period of the rise of Muslim rule in India mostly there were good rulers. There were certainly weaklings like Aram Shah, Ruknuddin Firoz Shah, Moizuddin Bahram Shah, Alauddin Masood Shah and Kaiqubbad of the slave dynasty. But there were also in the same family the good-natured and excellent administrators like Altutmish (better known as Ailtamash), of Balban's pomp and grandeur with equally excellent dispensation of justice, they took their empire to great heights of renown and power. Among the Khilji rulers there were drunkards like Qutbuddin Mubarak Shah and roguish usurpers like Naisruddin Khusro also, but the irregularities and corruptions of their period were over-shadowed by the earlier giant rulers, Alauddin's conquests and love of the subjects. The weaklings and incapable administrators damaged the interests of the dynasty but the kingdom survived. Nasiruddin's valour and wisdom, Muhammad bin Tughlaq's courage' and ambition and determination, and Firoz Shah's extraordinary kind-heartedness and generosity towards his subjects together made the kingdom so strong that even these weaker successors following them could be maintained in saddle for sometime. Ibrahim Lodi had to put up with the evil consequences of his weakness. The way Minhaj Siraj (compiler of *Tabqat-e-Firoz Shahi*) have been generous in mentioning the good qualities of Muslim monarchs, and in the same way the present day historians, Dr. K.S. Lal in his book "*History of the Khiljis*, Dr. Ishwari Parasad in his "*Politics in Pre-Mughal Times*", have also not been narrow minded or stingy in mentioning the good points of the praiseworthy kings.

The military genius and its marvellous performances, political, economic and cultural achievements of the first six Mughal emperors are so glorious that the last thirteen incapable and unworthy kings of their family remained in possession of their nominal kingdoms for a century and a half due to their fore-fathers having earned a renown surviving long after them and covering the faults of the weaklings and nincompoops. Nizamuddin Bakhshi in _Tabqat-e-Akbari_, Abul Fazl in _Akbar Namah_, Mustaid Khan in _Iqbal Namah Jahangiri_, Mulla Abdul Hameed Lahori in his _Badshahnama_, have lauded the praiseworthy kings, the Mughal emperors, among the present day historians, like Dr. Ram Prasad Tripathi in his "_History of Jahangir_", and Banarsi Parasad in his "_History of Shah Jahan_" have also paid tribute to these emperors, each one according to his own peculiar manner. However, in praise of Alamgir, the way the author of "_Alamgir Namah_", Kazmi Shirazi has unleashed his pen is unique and Sir Jadoo Nath Sarkar's pen appears to have been under very high reins in comparison. But of the lofty position of this (highly learned ascetic) emperor this argument suffices that a historian of the class of Jadoo Nath Sarkar in shrewdness and penetration, spent twenty years in writing out the history of this emperor in five volumes after much dilegent re-search. To date none has ever written the history of an "unworthy king" in so many volumes.

THE PECULIARITIES OF THE MUSLIM PERIOD

Who can deny the patent fact that during the Muslim rule in India many cultural and social splendours exhibited themselves. At the court and in the social life new manners and etiquettes got introduced which were adopted by the indigenous rulers, the petty Hindu rajahs of this country. In decoration and adornment, the beauty and elegance knew no bounds. In the patronage of sciences and arts great generosity was shown. There was great variation in dresses, cloth making industry progressed by leaps and bounds, brocade, velvet, atlas (Silk) Mushajjar, silk brocade (bida), muslin, soft woollen cloth, shawls, carpets and so on, were prepared in many styles. In making various kinds of ornaments great skill and fine workmanship began to be used. Jewels were heaped in plenty everywhere, (in crown, jewellery, cloth, in thrones and even in buildings). Outside new methods of embellishment and make-up were introduced. Musk, Amber, Lowan, Camphor, Zubad, Maid, Ud, Salaras, Loban, Mayah, Zafran (saffron) and many other scents were the sources of the preparation of exquisite perfumes. The arrangement of flowering plants in beds of various shapes in a garden, the experiments with these plants, grafting and other horticultural practices, import and introduction of these flowering plants and fruit trees into this tropical country from the colder climates (Afghanistan and Turkestan etc.) their former homelands and foreign to Indian soil, were some of the valuable contributions of Mughal emperors from Babar to Jahangir. Development of orchards and groves in such plenty in northen India is their tradition taken up and followed for centuries. Their own famous gardens in Delhi, Lahore and Kashmir, to mention just a few places, Shalimar, Lalazar and many other with beautiful names existed in good shape long after them, serving as witnesses to their fine tastes in this phase of life. Many new fruits were brought into existence as a result of cross-breeding and grafting as new additions in this field unknown in India before that. Victuals of so many kinds prepared with rice, wheat flour and meat and sweet dishes in the form of varieties of halwa, murabbas (fruits pickled in sugar solution), and numerous pickles, added to the variety and colourfulness in food items at the Indian table that is unsurpassed in the world even today. In architecture turnip shaped domes and many sided towers were introduced in India for the first time. Again in the engraving, enamelling, plastering, covering with glazed tiles, mosaic work, and patching or darning, the novelties created cannot be forgotten. Taj Mahal to this day is living witness to the fineness, exquisiteness and delicateness of the Mughal architectural art. In Music Amir Khusro, Tansen, Bax Bahadur, Bayazeed Khan, Sultan Zainul Abideen, Husain Shah Sharqi, Naik Bakhsu, Sultan Muzaffar Gujrati, Sultan Ibrahim Adil Shah Sani and Sultan Wajid Ali Shah's inventions to Indian Music are unforgettable. During the reigns of Akbar and Jahangir, the delicacy, mixing and use of colours, fineness, appropriate combination and emulating nature in painting that gave birth to a style which exists to this day by the name of Mughal art. It was due to his particular style that various schools of painting came into existence. Paper is the most valuable gift of the Muslim period to India. Rangpura, Ichah, Jaunpur, Ahmedabad, Ahmadnagar, Nimatabad, Burhanpur, Zainabad, Mubarkabad, Mustafabad, Daulatabad, Firozabad, Lahore, Allahabad, Agra, Fatehpur Sikri, Haidarabad, Muradabad, Aurangabad, Ibrahimabad, Azimabad, Bhakkar, Samanah and Allah alone knows better how many more cities, towns and villas sprang up during the Mughal period. Again, the bridges, roads and canals constructed by them were innumerable. The whole India was surveyed. Arable and non-arable lands were classified under different heads. Taqawi loans were offered to the poor cultivators, for digging wells, purchase of ploughs and oxen as also seed before the sowing season. It became an established system known as Taqawi system and continues to this day. Many different methods of assessment and collection were found out and applied to the different situations in the different parts of the country; and the soil (arable) was further classified from this point of view into Batai distribution of the produce between the owner and cultivator of the land on agreed terms), Barani (depending solely on rainfall for production), Chahi that could give produce if a well could be dug for irrigation), Nahri (irrigated with canal water) and the rest of it. No pains were spared in improving the local cattle for better breeds of milch and draught animals as well as providers of meat. The details can be looked up in the books of that period. Jadoo Nath Sarkar acknowledging the benevolent actions of Muslims has wirtten :

1. The Muslims became the means of the establishment of relations of India with the foreign

countries which helped growth and development of navigation in oceans and commerce through sea routes started anew. Our foreign relations were almost non-existant. **2.** In most part of India particularly those north of Vindhyachal, internal peace and security were established. **3.** A uniform system of governance created uniformity throughout the country. **4.** In spite of the differences in religious belief, the upper strata of society came to have a uniformity in habits, customs and manners and dress etc. and also in social affairs. **5.** An art of the Indian and Islamic style came into existence which combined also the Hindu and Chinese arts. This gave a certain shape to arthitecture and fine industries got accomplished. Shawls and carpets, brocade and lapidary are their memorable gifts to India. **6.** A common language came into existence which came to be Hindustani or Rekhtah. In prose wirting an official-style came into vogue initiated by Indians who used to write Persian. This style was emulated by Marathas also in their language. **7.** When due to the kingdom, based at Delhi, became the promoter of peace and prosperity, the literature also developed. **8.** In religion the concept of the unity of Allah was renewed and mysticism spread throughout the country. **9.** Historical literature was created. **10.** Military sciences and arts and the common department of culture developed. Jadoo Nath Sarkar also writes that it was due to Muslims that a new style was introduced and initiated in architecture. Palaces and Mausoleums are witness to their speciality in this field. Again they created a particular school of painting and it were they who created a taste and craving for orchards and groves.

HOW IS HISTORY DISTORTED

The Ex-Governor of Orissa, Mr. B.N. Pandey, in his lecture "Islam and Indian Culture" has said :

"Now I am going to present some such examples which will show how historical facts are distorted :

When I was busy in research on Tipu Sultan, at Allahabad University, some office bearers of the students union of Anglo Bengali College came to me with the request that I should inaugurate their history association. These student were coming direct from college and had their history text books also in their hands. By chance I happened to look at their history text books and opening the chapter on Tipu Sultan my gaze met this amazing sentence :

"Three thousand Brahmins committed suicide because Tipu Sultan wanted them to embrace Islam".

The author of this text book was Maha Mahupadhyay, Dr. Har Prasad Shastri, Chairman Department of Sanskrit, Calcutta University. I wrote at once to Dr. Shastri seeking his source of information about the above quoted statement. After repeated reminders I heard from him that he had picked up this information from Mysore Gazetteer. Mysore Gazetteer was neither available at Allahabad University Library nor in Imperial Library Calcutta. Then I wrote to the then Vice-Chancellor, Mysore University, Sir. Bijendra Nath Sail, seeking verification of Shastri's statement. He sent my letter to Professor Sri Kantayya who was at the time handling a fresh edition of Mysore Gazeteer for printing a new edition.

Professor Kantayya wrote to me that the incident of the suicide of three thousand Brahmins is nowhere to be found in the Mysore Gazetteer. And he, himself as a student of Mysore history, can say with confidence that such an incident never happened. He also wrote that Tipu's prime minister was a Brahmin Purnayya by name and the Commander of his forces was also a Brahmin, Krishan Rao. He sent me a list of 156 temples that were the recipients of annual grants from Tipu Sultan. He also sent thirty photo-copies of letters written by Tipu Sultan to the Jagat Guru Shankaracharya of Sarangeri Math with whom the Sultan was on very friendly terms. According to the tradition of the rulers of Mysore, Tipu used to visit Ranga Nathji's temple before breakfast every morning. This temple was in the Srirangapatnam fort. According to Professor Kantayya's guess, Dr. Shastri must have borrowed his material from Col. Moyal's so called book "History of Mysore" This author claims to have translated his book from a Persian manuscript found in Queen Victoria's personal library. On a searching enquiry it was found that there was no such manuscript in the Queen's library, and most of the statements of Colonel Moyal are false and farbricated.

Dr. Shastri's book was the approved text book for Bengal. Assam, Bihar, Orissa, U.P., Madhya Pradesh and Rajasthan. I sent the copies of all the correspondence in this connection to Shri Ashutosh Chaudhari, the then Vice Chancellor of Calcutta University requesting him to take appropriate action against this statement in Shastri's book. Shri Ashutosh replied promptly that Shastri's above mentioned book has been excluded from the syllabus.

But I was amazed to find that the same incident of suicide of three thousand Brahmins was very much there in 1972 in the Junior High School history text books in U.P.

Mahatam Gandhi's 'Young India' the issue of 23rd January 1938, on page 31 carried the following critical note :

'Mysore's Fateh Ali Tipu Sultan has been presented by the foreigners as an extremist who tyrannized his Hindu subjects and compelled them to embrace Islam, when the facts were just the opposite. His relation with his Hindu subjects were most agreeable, ...Mysore's department of Archaeology has three letters in its possession written to Sarangerinath's Jagat Guru Shankaracharya, in 1793. In one of these letters, he (Sultan), acknowledging the receipt of Shankaracharya's letter, has requested him to pray for him and for the whole world's well-being and prosperity. In the end he has requested the Shankaracharya to return to Mysore since the presence of a good man invites rain at any palce. The crops are good and thus there is an all round reign of prosperity. This letter deserves to be written in letters of gold in the history of India.

Tipu conferred valuable gifts on Hindu temples, particularly Shri Venkat Ramana, Shri Niwas and Shri Ranganath temples in the form of land and other things. Some temples stood even in his palaces. This is living proof of his open mindedness and tolerance in the extreme, and brings out the fact that his martyr who must be declared a martyr of the struggle of freedom never complained of any disturbance in his own prayer due to the noise of bells of the Hindu temples in his own palaces. Tipu fell to the enemy's bullets fighting valiantly for freedom and turned down with contempt the offer of laying down arms before the enemy. When Tipu's dead body was discovered among the dead, it was seen that even after death his grip on his sword had not relaxed - the sword that was the means of winning freedom from foreign rule and slavery'. His last words on the occasion of his confrontation are memorable indeed : "One day of lion's fearless life (of freedom) is better than the hundred years' life of a fox (spent in deadly fear of the mighty)." The last strain of a poem eulogising him is also worth remembering, which says : "To die under the cloud pouring blood in a battle field is much better than to live a life of ingominy and degradation".

Similarly when I was the Chairman of the Allahabad Municipality (1948-1953), a case of 'Dakhilkharij', (proceedings of the transfer of property to the new proprietor), was put up before me. This contention was about Someshwarnath Mahadev Mandir relating to property. After the death of the temple's mahant, there were two claimants to this endowments. One of them, (claimants), presented in proof of his claim some documents that had been in possession of the family. These documents were Emperor Aurangzeb's firmans (edicts). Aurangzeb had given to the temple landed property as free grant and cash as gifts. I thought to myself that these edicts must be false fabrications. How could Aurangzeb, notorious for demolition of temples, could have given a jagir to a Hindu temple, specifying that it was for puja (worship) and Bhog (food offered to the idols). How could he possibly have anything to do with idol worship?

I was sure that the documents were forged. But before arriving at any decision in this regard, I deemed it fit to take them to Dr. Sir Tej Bahadur Sapru for his opinion. He was a great scholar of Persian and Arabic. Putting up the documents before him I asked for his opinion about them. After careful examination of these documents, he said, "These edicts of Aurangzeb are genuine and real. Then he ordered his clerk to bring the file of Jangambari Shiv Mandir to him. In connection with this case there had been several appeals, under hearing at the Allahabad High Court for the last fifteen years. The mahant of this mandir too had several edicts of jagirs to the temple.

This was a new picture of Aurangzeb that had come up before me totally different from the one painted by his blind critics in their religious zeal. I was simply amazed. According to the advice of Dr. Sapru, sending letter to several important temples throughout India, I requested the mahants that in case of having with them any edicts of Aurangzeb granting jagirs to the temples, they should kindly send their photo-copies to me. Once again I experienced the same amazement when I received the photo-copies of Aurangzeb's edicts granting jagirs and other gifts to Mahakaleshwar mandir of Ujjain, Jain mandir of Shatrunjai and many other great mandirs and gurudwaras spread over northern India. These edicts had been issued from 1659 to 1685 A.D. (1065-1091 A.H.)

Although with regard to Hindus and their temples, Aurangzeb's open-mindedness became evidenced from these few examples, but they are enough to prove conclusively that the writings of historians about him are based on prejudice and religious hatred. In this popular portrait only one side of his character has been painted. India is such a vast country with thousands of Hindu temples spread all over. If properly investigated, I am sure many more such examples of his broad mindedness and open heartedness shall be found, furnishing proof of Aurangzeb's generous treatment of the non-Muslims of his Indian empire.

In connection with the investigation of the edicts of Aurangzeb I came in contact with Shri Gyan Chandra and D.P.L. Gupta, Ex-curator of Patna Museum. These gentlemen too were busy in research on important points about Aurangzeb. I was pleased to see that some other investigators too are in search of truth and are occupied with their share in untarnishing the portrait of Aurangzeb - Aurangzeb whom the prejudiced historians have declared to be the symbol of Muslim rule in India, so much so that a poet (like Shibli, a historian and investigator in his own right) had to say : "All that you remember in the whole story is only this (much), that Aurangzeb was hostile to Hindus, a tyrant and an oppressor."

A firman (edict) of his has been very much tossed up (propagated) with regard to Aurangzeb's hostility to Hindus, which goes by the name of Firman-e-Banaras. This firman is about a Brahmin family of Gori Mohallah of Banaras. In 1905 it was presented to the city magistrate by Gopi Upadhyay's grandson, Mangal Sen. It was first published by the Asiatic Society Bengal's journal in 1911, and became the centre of interest of researchers. From that time onward the historians have been frequently referring to it, and on its basis they accuse Aurangzeb of having banned construction of new Hindu temples. Where as the real importance of this firman remains hidden from their (highly prejudiced) view.

This firman was issued by Aurangzeb on 15 Jamadi I, 1065 A.H. / March 1659 to the governor of Banaras on the complaint of a Brahmin. He (the Brahmin) was a trustee and treasurer of a temple and some people were harassing him. The firman says :

"In recognition of our royal favours to him, Abul Hasan must know that in keeping with our kindness and natural justice the aim and object of all our untiring efforts and the institutions of justice, established by us, is to make public welfare an accomplished fact and to improve the conditions of the lower classes of society. According to our revered law we have decided that the old standing temples should not be destroyed or demolished. However, new temples should not be constructed.

In this period of justice of ours the news has found its way to our honoured and revered court that some people are giving trouble to and harassing the Hindu citizens of Banaras and its neighbourhood and also Brahmin Prohits and meddling in their affairs, whereas the old temples are under their supervision. Moreover, they (the mischief mongers and the meddling lot) want to oust the Brahmin from their time-honoured posts. This interference is a source of vexation for this community (Brahmins).

Therefore it is our commandment that immediately, on receipt of our orders, you should issue instructions that no one should meddle in these affairs unlawfully and should abstain from harassing Brahmins of these places as also other Hindu citizens, so that they may remain in possession of them (their posts of old) and they may go on praying in the state of full satisfaction, for the well being of this kingdom of ours, conferred on us by Allah and destined to last until the end of days. Take these orders from us as immediate for compliance.

This firman is quite explicit with regard to the fact that Aurangzeb had not issued any new orders against construction of new temples but had only referred to a practice in vogue long since and stressed compliance with that order. He strictly forbade destruction of the existing temples. The firman also makes it evident that he was eager to provide an atmosphere in which opportunity for Hindu subject to make a peaceful and happy life easy for them.

This is not the only firman of its type. Another came to light (also) in Banaras which shows that Aurangzeb was really desirous of it that Hindus should be able to live peacefully. The firman runs like this :

Raja Ram Singh, maharaj adhiraj of Ramnagar

(Banaras) has put up an application in our durbar that his father had a house built for the residence of his religious teacher, Bhagwat Goshaeen on the bank of river Ganges. Now some people are harassing the Goshaeen. So in this behalf this firman is being issued that immediately on receipt of it the present administrative officers and those following them should devote full attention to the fact that no one should be able to harm the Goshaeen, nor should anyone meddle in his affairs including his stay there, so that they may be praying for the welfare and maintenance and permanence of our God given kingdom. This should be taken as a matter of immediate importance.

(Dated Rabi II, 1091 A.H.)

The firman in possession of Jangambari math reveals that Aurangzeb could never tolerate it that the rights of his subjects should be trodden under foot, irrespective of their religion, Islam or Hinduism. He dealt harshly with the criminals. In a firman of this type the complaint of the followers of Jangam sect against a Muslim, Nazeer Beg, at the durbar of Aurangzeb has come for mention. And then issuing orders it has been said that the attention of the officers of Banaras in the province of Allahabad is drawn to it that the residents of Parganah Banaras, Arjun Mal and the Jangamis have brought this complaint to our royal notice that a resident of Banaras, Nazeer Beg, has illegally taken possession of five of their havelies (houses). They, the administrative officers are ordered that if they find the complaint true, and the right of the possession of the property is established, Nazeer Beg should not be allowed to enter those havelies (usurped houses) so that Jangamis may not have to approach our durbar again for redressal. This firman bears the date Shaban 11, 13th of July 1672 A.D.. Another firman in possession of the same math bears the date 1 Rabi I, 1078 A.H. saying that the posession of this land by Jangamis has been maintained.

It is announced for the benefit of the present and the succeeding jagirdars and Krovis of Parganah Haveli Banaras that under orders of the emperor 178 bighas of land has been conferred on Jangamis. The earlier administrators had verified and allowed it and the present holder of office of the Parganah has attested the complaint with his signature (seal) that the land belongs to them. So it was given to them as alms to the poor for the well being of the emperor. The possession should take effect from the beginning of Fasle Kharif (summer and rainy season crop). And no further meddling with it be allowed in future so that the jagir may go on providing a living for them from its produce.

This firman does not only reveal that justice was an essential element of his (Aurangzeb's) nature, but it is also evident from it that in this type of endowments of jagirs he never discriminated in conferring them on Hindu engaged in religious service. This jagir, 178 bighas of free grant of land had probably been conferred on Jangamis by Aurangzeb himself, since in another firman dated 5, Ramadhan 1017 A.H., it has been clearly stated that this land is free of land revenue.

Aurangzeb through another firman (dated 1098

A.H.) had also endowed another Hindu religious institution with landed property. The firman says:

Two plots of land are lying vacant on Beni Madho Ghat on river Ganges in Banaras. One of them is by the side of markazi masjid opposite the house of Ramjiwan Goshaeen, and the other a little behind it. These plots are the property of Bait-ul-Mal (public exchequer). We gave them away to Ramjiwan Goshaeen and his son, as a gift, so that after building residential quarters on the plots for Brahmins and ascetics, and thus peacefully settled they may remain busy in worship and prayer for the maintenance and well-being of our God-given kingdom. Our sons, ministers, nobles and high officials daroghahs, and the present and succeeding kotwals should take it as their bounden duty to see to it compliance, letting the said plot remain in possession of the said person and his heirs. Neither any land revenue be demanded from them nor annual renewal of the grant, be made obligatory.

It appears Aurangzeb had great regard and respect for the religious feelings of his subjects. We have another firman of Aurangzeb, dated 2 Safar, 9th year of Julus, (Coronation). It is addressed to Sudaman Brahmin of Umanand temple of Gauhati in Assam. A plot of land and income of a certain tract of forest wealth, had been conferred on the temple and its priest, so that the expenses of Bhog may be met and the priest may subsist on it. When the province fell into the hands of Aurangzeb, he at once confirmed the temple endowment.

Further proof of Aurangzeb's tolerant attitude is

provided by the statement of the priests of Mahakaleshwar temple in Ujjain. This is one of the most important Shiv temples where a lamp is continually kept burning - day and night. Four seers of ghee daily was provided by the rulers of yore. Pujaris say that this practice continued during the Mughal period also, and Aurangzeb also respected this old tradition. Unfortunately the priests have no firman to this effect but they certainly have a copy of an order which had been issued by Prince Murad Bakhsh during Aurangzeb's regime (dated 5 Shawwal 1061 A.H). This order had been issued by the prince on behalf of the emperor at the request of the temple priest, Dev Narain. After the verification of Waqai Nawis (reporters of the news to the royal court), it had been said in this order that for the lamp of the temple, the tahsildar of the Chabootra Kotwal should supply four seers ghee per day (according to the Akbari weights) constantly. A copy of it, ninety three years after the issue of the original in 1153 A.H. was re-issued by Muhammad Sadullah.

The historians frequently mention that the Chintaman mandir in Ahmedabad built by Nagarnath was demolished. But they craftily conceal the fact that this very Aurangzeb had endowed the Shitrunji temple built by the same Nagar Nath Seth with jagirs liberally.

Undoubtedly history goes to prove that Aurangzeb had ordered demolition of Vishwanath temple at Banaras and the Jami Masjid of Golkunda. But there were other reasons for it. The story of Vishwa Nath temple is this that Aurangzeb on his way to Bengal was passing by Banaras when the Hindu rajahs of his entourage requested that if the royal carvan could stop its onward march for a day their ranis would have taken a holy dip in Ganges at Banras and also pay their homage at the Vishwanath temple. Aurangzeb at once granted their request and from the place of royal sojourn upto Banaras, a distance of four or five miles, he ordered appointment of military guards for the safety of the ranis and their entourage. The Ranis covered this distance in palkis (planquins) and returned after their bath in Ganges and visit to the temple, but one of them (the Maharani of Kuchh) could not be traced inspite of search of the premises. When Aurangzeb came to know about it, he got infuriated and sent his senior officers for further investigation. They, after some careful observation noticed that the idol of Ganesh fixed to the wall moves on manipulation. They got it removed from the fixed spot and discovered a staircase descending into a basement. And the lost Rani was found there (in the dark basement) dishevelled, with a frightened look and weeping piteously. She had been raped there by the priests and her jewellery had been forcibly taken from her. This basement was just below the idol of Vishwanath. The rajahs showed great ire and put up a protest. Since a very heinous crime had been perpetrated, they demanded a very strict action against the culprits. In keeping with their demand Aurangzeb ordered that since the sanctity of the sacred spot had been trampled with impunity the idol of Vishwanath should be transferred to some other spot and installed there, the temple razed to the ground, and the mahant (the priest) be arrested.

Dr. Pattebhi Sitaramayyah, in his book, "The Feathers and Stools" has recorded this incident with documentary evidence and it has been further testified by the excurator of Patna Museum, Dr. P.L. Gupta.

The incident of the Jama Masjid of Golkunda runs like this that the ruler of the state after realization of revenues did not pay the amount of tribute to Delhi. In a few years time, it mounted to a fabulous sum (crores of rupees). Tana Shah the ruler of Golkunda, burried this treasure and built a mosque over it. When Aurangzeb got news of this mischief, he ordered demolition of that mosque. The treasure was dug out and spent on public welfare. These two examples are enough to show that in matters of meting out justice Aurangzeb never discriminated between a temple and a mosque.

Unfortunately the events of medieval as well as modern history is being so much distorted, according to the historians own liking and taste, that falsehood alone has come to be believed like the true word of Allah. And those who try to differentiate between reality and myths, and falsehood and truth, are accused in various ways. The communalists, the self-seeking and those with vested interests have been busy in destroying history and giving it a false hue, and are just as active today if not more."

THE PROBLEM OF THE PLACES OF WORSHIP

The Britishers, since they had fully understood the fact that the Indian masses are passionately attached to religion, to create a gulf between the Hindus and Muslims they used religion as the most effective weapon. They vehemently launched a rather blatant propaganda that the

Muslim rulers during their period of authority and rule continued building mosques in place of the temples that they were never tired of demolishing and with relish too. And it is on the basis of books written by these colonizers (the Britishers) that many of the Hindu historians too have started talking in that strain, whereas the Muslim rulers were hardly ever free from the all-occupying business of coming into power and authority and the constant vigilance in maintaining it, to think of other 'futile pursuits.' Where Islam is concerned, it has time and again stressed the sancity of the places of worship of other religions, not at all permitting to damage or demolish them under any conditions whatsoever, not to say of permitting erecting mosques on the sites of demolished temples. That is why the Muslims have ever been very careful in building mosques (since building them on forcibly snatched, usurped land is strictly prohibited - no lawful possession of land no mosque). Syed Sabahuddin Abdur Rahman, of late lamented memory, says in his book "Babari Masjid": Building a mosque on usurped land is totally disallowed, and if built, it will have to be demolished. For building a mosque Ulama and jurists have laid down so many conditions without fulfilment of which they do not issue the permit of its validity and soundness. In the opinion of jurists the mosque built for show or for self-aggrandisement or any other vicious objective and having little or no consideration of seeking objective and having little or no consideratrion of seeking the countenance of Allah, or one built with illgotten wealth, is like masjide "Zorar" (*Tafseerat-e-Ahmadi*, p. 283, *Madarik Alal Khazin*, Vol.

II, p. 265). It means that such a mosque is not that of the Muslims but the hypocrites.

It is also the opinion of the jurists that if a person builds a mosque at a place where somebody else has a right and his consent has not been previously obtained the person with claim to it has a right of neighbourhood or one of pre-emplion, a mosque cannot be built on such a piece of land, (Fathul Qadeer, Vol. II, p. 875). Similarly a person is sick or it is his earnest desire to change his house into a mosque, or he even willed it at the time of his death but his rightful heirs (inheritors) do not acknowledge his will, that will shall be declared null and void (*Fatawa Alamgiri* Vol. II, p. 456). Similarly a plot of land purchased in a prohibited manner of purchase is not fit for building a mosque. It is disallowed (*Fathul Qadeer*, Vol. II, p. 875). An unlawfully obtained plot of land is no good for building a mosque on, no matter what the shape of the unlawful possession. For example some people may convert somebody's house into a mosque or Jami Masjid, it will not be permissible to say prayers in such a mosque. (*Fatawa Alamgiri* Vol. VI, p. 214). Or there may be a public road which becomes difficult to use or damaging it by building a mosque, it will not be permissible to build such a mosque (*Fatawa Alamgiri* Vol. III, p. 229). Acquisition of land by lawful method has been explained thus that there should be nobody's claim to it. It has been said in *Hidayah* (the authentic book of Islamic laws) that if a person builds a mosque with a basement below and residential space above it and mosque between the two and its entrance and outlet open on a public road, under these conditions even if he has given up possession of the mosque and endowed it for prayers, it will not be proper, for when he has not sold it in a regular transaction, he himself or his lawful inheritors shall retain the right to sell it. The writer of *Hidayah* has rationally explained it in this way that this mosque was not purely and exclusively surrendered to Allah since it has man's right attached to it yet. The general principle is this that the mosque is that structrure over which no one has any right of interference, meaning that there should be nobody's right in any way whatsoever (*Hidayah* Vol. II, p. 625). The recent compilations of Fatawah or verdicts of Shariah also have such examples. For example in *Fatawa Rizviyah* in response to an enquiry it has been said that the mosques are for Allah alone. Therefore it is necessary that they should be totally free from all claims of the servants of Allah to it. If the property of man remains in some portion of the mosque, it will not be a mosque.

(Fatawa Rizviyah Vol. VI, p. 453).

Similarly an enquiry read like this: The Muslims want to purchase land from a Hindu Zamindar for building a mosque, since the Muslims have no piece of land, more than their inherited holdings, over which a mosque or a congregational mosque (Jama Masjid) could be built. But that Hindu zamindar is not prepared to sell his land to Muslims (for the construction of a mosque). What is the way out of this difficulty for us? The following verdict was received in reply to this query of Muslims: "If that Hindu Zamindar does not want to sell his land, the Muslims should say their prayers in their houses.

(*Fatawa Rizviyah* Vol. VI, p. 661). Similarly, if the land is the joint property (of the Muslims and the government), building a mosque on it without government's permission is not allowed. And if such a mosque is built at all saying prayers in that mosque will harldy benefit anyone. Rather, prayers should not be said there. (*Majmua Fatawa* Maulvi Abdul Hai, with reference to Mufti Muhammad Kafi, p. 25). Similarly, construction of a mosque on land belonging to a minor is not permitted. (Supplement to *Imdadul Fatawa* with reference to *Adabul-Masajid*, Mufti Muhammad Shafi, p. 25). A mosque built by a dissolute woman with her earnings of sin, it will not be accepted as a mosque at all. And she shall not be entitled to any benefit in the Hereafter.

(*Majmuah Fatawa Maulana Abdul Hai*, p. 268).

When there are so many restrictive conditions for building a mosque, how is it possible that Muslims and their rulers might have been building mosques on the ruins of their own demolished temples? In the foregoing pages it has been clearly stated that for building a mosque land acquired by lawful means only can be utilised, when it is known for certain that nobody's rights have been usurped in its acquirement, nor any pressure or force was used in its acquisition. How can demolition of a temple and building a mosque on its site could be permitted to them. It is possible that during the fury of a war and conditions of extreme hostility, the Muslims might have demolished a temple, or finding a temple a centre of conspiracies, rebellion or lewdness and debauchery, it might have been toppled. But building a mosque on the remains of a demolished temple cannot be imagined, not to say of 'proved'. And supposing a hot-tempered crazy with war-fury conqueror did build a mosque of this type, the ulama, the jurists and the common people behind them, could never accept it as a mosque. It is also possible to conjecture that a mosque might have been built at a little distance from the ruins of temples of yore, but never one was built on the very site of a temple purposely demolished for it.

The Britishers during their period of rule in India certainly tried to spread this baseless and nonsensical information or disinformation as it should be called. But they had no norms of morality in these matters where political gains and vested interests came in. Their interest in ruling over India peacefully lay in making Hindus and Muslims run at each other's throat, in which they succeeded marvellously by distorting history and poisoning the minds of Hindus against the Muslims and their rulers in the immediate past. However, an unbiased person can think over it and conclude for himself that if destruction and demolition of Hindu temples had been the mission of Muslim rulers in India as a matter of creed, during such a lengthy period of their authority and rule (spread over centuries with a strong military force at their back which could accomplish anything) not one temple from Kashmir to Cape Comorin and from Punjab to Assam would have been allowed to stand on its foundation. Could Jain Mandir facing the gate of red fort been allowed to stand where it does today ? It is very much there to falsify the absurd allegations of yesterday and today......

Hindu historians with a clean and unbiased mind acknowledge that the temples demolished during the Muslim regime were either centres of rebellion and conspiracies or perpetration of heinous crimes by unlawful means through middlemen exploitation and of the devotees, particularly easily moved weaker gullible sex. Dr. Ishwar Topa has written in his book '_Politics in Pre-Mughal Times_', that during the period of Firoz Tughlaq some temples were the centres of immorality. In the fairs arranged under the auspices of the temple, Hindus and Muslims both participated. Women also adorned these fairs by arrangement. So the temples instead of being the centres of worship and devotion had become devoted to devilry. Firoz Shah under Islamic and moral sentiments got these seats of demoralizing satanic activities demolished. It is a different question altogether, whether Firoz Shah had any lawful right to improve the morality of his subjects or not, the fact is that whatever Firoz Shah did, religious fervour denigratingly called Fund-mentalism in today's parlance. It was taken in good faith and as a good turn to his subjects that he had tried to rectify their morality. If he had any tendency to destroy centres of polytheism, he would have made short shrift of them in no time. But he did not do any such thing. He had in view the rights of zimmis in an Islamic or Muslim state and maintenance and protection of the Hindu temples was part of those rights" (p. 247).

That makes it amply evident that the Hindu temples

that got demolished during the period of Muslim rule in India was not for the reason that they were Hindu places of worship but for other reasons which deserve careful and critical examination with an unprejudiced mind. Aurangzeb is declared to be the great villain in the practice of temple demolition. The five volumes written by Jadoonath Sarkar on Aurangzeb at the instigation of his British masters has left no stone unturned in the display of his temple demolition "craze". His pen vigorous normally also, becomes unleashed in giving details. He writes that during his princely period and that of monarchy, he had got demolished Saraspur, Chintaman, Ahmedabad, Satara (a village of Aurangabad,) Somnath, Vishwanath of Banaras, Kesurai mandir of Mathura and Ujjain mandir. They are not more than twelve or thirteen in number. Jadoonath mentions the demolition of these temples in such a way (that it may appear) Aurangzeb had made up his mind to demolish all the temples of India. But he never got demolished any temple of his capital towns, Delhi and Agra. But wonder of wonders is the fact that he spent twenty five years of his life in Deccan where Ajanta and Elora stand intact to this day, and a couple of miles from his last resting place, he never for a moment thought of destroying them. Rather his court historian and author of *Ma'athir-e-Alamgiri* praises them (Ajanta and Elora) by calling them 'pleasing to the eye.'
(Maathir-e-Alamgiri, p.338).

Again, when temple demolition is made the topic, demolition of mosques should also come for mention with equal zeal (or at least as simple statements of facts of history). People have a right to know how many of them (mosques) were martyred by zealots among Hindus. During the period of Jahangir and Shah Jahan, at the height of their power, in Gujarat, Hindus after demolishing the mosques, had come to use them as their habitations. (*Badshahnamah*, Abdul Hameed, Lahori, Vol. II, p. 57). When Ali Adil Shah called Raja Ram of Bijanagar in 976 A.H. to his aid against Nizam Shah Habri, Raja Ram burnt up all the mosques of Ali Adil Shah's kingdom. -(*Tarikh-e-Farishta*, Vol. II, p.36, Lucknow edition). Jadoonath Sarkar has himself confessed that during the period of Aurangzeb the Satnamis after plundering Narnol demolished all its mosques, (History of Aurangzeb, Zaheeruddin Faruqi, p. 134). After the death of Bahadur Shah I, the successor of Aurangzeb, Ajit Singh, son of Raja Jaswant Singh of Jodhpur, got demolished mosques of Jodhpur, and had temples built on their sites (*Muntakhabul Lubab*, Kafi Khan, Vol. II, p. 231). The Sikh, in their period of authority and rule damaged and destroyed thousands of mosques. It is a story separate from the one under discussion. (For details see History of Lahore by Kanahya Lal Kapoor, p. 135-152). After 1947 the desecration and destruction of mosques can still be witnessed (fifty years after the holocaust). In 1976 the government had appointed Barni Committee. Its report stated that upto the time of reporting there were 176 mosques in Delhi, which Muslims could not use for their prayers. They were either under the surveillance of the government or Hindu public, and have not so far been released and handed over to the Muslims. Delhi had been the Capital of Muslim rulers of India. But on no reliable authority it can be proved that Hindus here in the Capital of India have ever been deprived of their 176 temples. In 1979 in Bengal Assembly in reply to a question it was given out that in Calcutta alone 59 mosques have been made inaccessible to Muslims and are in the possession of Hindus. Some of them are defiled by plastering the floor and walls with cow-dung after the manner of Hindu villagers. No history of Indian Muslims can furnish evidence of desecration of 59 temples at one place. And on the other side the news papers have been vociferous in announcing that from Delhi to Pakistan frontier nine thousand mosques are under the control of Hindus.

The fact is that revolutions bring with them many destructive forces and ruinations. So in wars and during the changes of hands of authority and rule such unpleasant incidents cannot be called unusual. But the important thing is this that after the storm has abated and emergency gives way to a situation of normalcy and stability injustices must be revoked.

TOLERANCE OF THE MUSLIM RULERS

Babar writes in his will to his son Humayun : My son! The empire of India is replete with different religions. Gratitude is due to Allah that He conferred it on us. It is binding on you that you should do away with all the religious prejudices and dispense justice to them according to the dictates of their own religions. In particular give up cow-slaughter even for sacrificial purposes. You will thereby win the hearts of the people of this land. The subjects of this country shall be obliged to you under the sense of gratitude to the rulers. The people who obey the laws of the government of the land, You should not tamper with their temples and other places of worship. Dispense justice in a manner so that the king may remain pleased with his subjects and the subjects with the ruler. Islam can be propagated and spread much better with the sword of favours and beneficence than with the sword of tyranny. The difference of Sunnis and Shiahs must be overlooked or else Islam shall become weak. The subjects with different beliefs should be so beautifully brought together as the various elements in a body remain together in proper combination may remain free from differences and factions.

(India Divided, p. 39 IIIrd edition).

Professor Sri Ram Sharma has written in his book *"Mughal Empire of India"* on p. 55 : "We do not come upon any evidence to show that Babar demolished any temple or gave trouble to any Hindu for the reason that he was a Hindu.

Pandit Jawahar Lal Nehru has written about him that his personality was very charming. He was a leader of the period of renaissance. He was very brave and daring. He was very fond of Art, literature and a life of cheerfulness, luxury and comfort. Humayun also kept his people inclined to himself. And the tolerance of Sher Shah shall be appreciated and lauded in every age. He had created such an agreeable combination of religion and polity that had brought into existence very appropriate and favourable atmosphere for Hindustani Qaumyat (Indian Nationality). Both the British and Hindu historians are one on the fact that he is the first ruler of India who tried to lay the foundation of an Indian empire according to the general will. And this feat he performed disgressing from that period's political principles that since political union is not possible without riligious uniformity. He did not like to be narrow-minded.

Therefore he did not like that his own community alone should regard themselves deserving of participation in authority and rule, but remain loyal to him keeping in view the common interests of the entire populace. In this way he paved the way for the coming into existence of an Indian Nation. Among the present day historians Kalkaranjan Qanungo, the author of "*Sher Shah*" has written :

"Sher Shah is the first ruler, who, bringing together the followers of various religions tried to shape some sort of an Indian nation. This distinction goes to Akbar and for Sher Shah this claim appears to be rather misappropriate, since on the surface of it, he did not abstain from realizing Jizyah from the Hindu zimmis. He did not enact any law prohibiting cowslaughter. He did not partonize Sanskrit language, so as to create a cultural and learning unity between Hindus and Muslims. He did not try either to establish matrimonial relations between Hindus and Muslims. And all these things are attributed to Akbar. But Sher Shah was a statesman in the real sense. He never tried to build a castle in the air, through the magical effects of Alladin's lamp, but established such a strong, stable and just system of governance which brought political and economic prosperity to the kingdom in the natural course. He prepared both Hindus and Muslims to come together and remain united, and all those things necessary for this purpose he had to put into practice".

Mr. T.W. Arnold has quoted an incident, relating to Aurangzeb in his book, "*Dawat-e-Islam*".

"One of the mansabdars of Aurangzeb, Ameen Khan susbmitted an aplication that two Parsi government servants be dismissed from service since they are Majusi (fireworshippers) and should be replaced by two reliable and experienced Muslims since the Quran says :

"O ye who believe' Take not my enemies and yours as friends (or protectors).

(Al-Quran LX : 1)

Aurangzeb wrote his order on this application :

"Religion has nothing to do with wordly affairs. Nor can prejudice find a place in those matters. And in support of his statement he cited the following Quranic verse :

"To you be your way and to me mine.(Q. CIX : 6)

The verse quoted by the applicant had it meant what he has understood, we ought to have destroyed (wasted) the rajahs of this country and their subjects. But how is it possible? The government services shall be given to those who are competent for them and not on any other basis".

The famous learned person from Bengal, Sir C.P. Roy, in a meeting of Bengal Muslim in Federation in 1937, had said in his presidential address :

"During the regime of Aurangzeb, Bengali Hindus were the recipients of mansabdari and large landed properties and they were made big Zamidars. Aurangzeb made Hindus governors, governor generals and even viceroys, taking it to that extreme where in a purely Islamic province, Afghanistan, the person who was appointed viceroy, was a Hindu Rajput".

Pandit Sunder Lal had written in 1936 in a paper of his "*Bharat men Aurangzeb Raj*" :

"During the period of Akbar, Jehangir, Shahjahan and after them Aurangzeb and all his successors, Hindus and Muslims had similar status. Both the religions were respected equally, and no partiality on the basis of religion was ever noticed in any-body's case. From everyone of them it was fair play. From every one of those kings the priests of innumerable temples were endowed with jagirs and free-grant lands. Aurangzeb's firmans bearing his signature (seal of authority) are with so many priests of Hindu temples even today, mentioning the endowment of Jagirs and lands free of revenue. Two such firmans are still to be found at Allahabad, one of which is with the priests of Someshwar Nath temple)"

It has been vehemently published that Aurangzeb had dismissed Hindus from high offices in his government. But the details given by Allamah Shibli Nomani in his article "*Aurangzeb Alamgir par ek Nazar*", Hindus in sufficiently large numbers are found holding important posts : For example :

Shash Hazari	(Holidng charge of six thousand armed men).	Three
Panj Hazari	(Five thousand armed men under his charge).	Nine
	Among whom Shivaji's son-in-law Arjunji and Malavji Bhonsle are prominent.	
Chahar Hazari	(Having charge of four thousand men).	Thirteen
	Including Shivaji's son-in-law Naththu.	
Do Hazar aur Panj Sad Hazari	(Charge holder of two thousand and five hudred).	Nine
Do Hazari	(Having under his control two thousand men).	Five
Yak Hazar aur Panj Sad Hazari	(Having under him only fifteen thousand men).	Four
Yak Hazari	(Only one thousand armed men).	Eight
Haft Sadi mansabdar	(Seven hundred men) only one	
Panj Sadi mansabdar	(In command of Five hundred men).	One
Yak Sadi mansabdar	(Only a hudred armed men).	One

Moreover forty-one more names are mentioned in history who are said to be holding very high posts in Aurangzeb's government. Shivaji's grandson, Sahukar — whose father Sambha Rao who had been severely punished by Aurangzeb and put to death — had been the receipient of a mansab, a post having seven thousand fighting men under his command. The title of Rajah was also conferred on him. With Sahu his relationship was always one of extreme generosity and partonage. So when after Aurangzeb's death, Sahu held aloft the banner of independence, he still had so much regard for his emperor Aurangzeb's favours that after declaratioin of independence as a rajah, the first thing that he did was to visit the grave of Aurangzeb at Aurangabad. (*Maathir-ul-Umara*, Vol II, p. 351)

Bombay Chronicle had wirtten an article in 1918 about Tipu Sultan : "Tipu's portrait has been presented to us in such a way that he was an extremely despotic ruler. Nothing could please him so much as shedding the blood of a non-Muslim. If he could, he would have totally eliminated Hinduism from South India. But now we are in possession of authoritative documents which are related to Sarangari math. And they attach no value to those things which our earlier authors had been teaching on this subject. These letters which have passed between the religious office of Shankraacharya's successors and Haider Ali and Tipu Sultan, deserve to be printed separately and further explained. In the light of these letters it becomes possible, and which is essential also, that these relations should be studied together and their nature determined so as to fully understand the nature of relations between the Muslim rulers and the Hindu religious leaders, and which is a matter of recent past. We are thankful to those Hindu revered personages who permitted careful examination and translation of 28 letters of Tipu Sultan. Every one of these letter provides witness to the honour and dignity which these Hindu leaders enjoyed in the esteem of this "despotic ruler". In some letters this Muslim king requests the Hindu priests to pray for the well being of his own and that of his kingdom and that they should bless them. These written notes or memoranda have a great importance of their own from another angle also. They are not only a strong argument in support of the fact that the relations between the followers of those two religions were no less agreeable. Rather, it is also a fact that the breach of peace between them was not due to religious but secular reasons which got the better of religious understandings and compromises. The fact is that a Hindu if he was not in agreement with a Muslim it was on the same basis on which he differed from a Hidnu brother. If the Marhattas damaged and demolished the mosques it was not for the reason that they were the religious sacred places of worship of Muslims but that they were edifies which their enemies cherished. Marhattas dismantled Hindu temples with the same vehemence and vigour which they exhibited in the demolition of Muslim mosques. The Swami of Sarangari math complains to Tipu about the barabarity and blood thirstiness of Marhattas which they exhibited in robbing their temples. He also requests the king for money and material for the repairs of the damaged idols which had been badly damaged by the

Marhattas in their fury. Tipu neither rejects this request of the Hindus nor gloats over the religious battles between two groups of non-Muslim.

Tipu in his royal edict quotes a piece of Sanskrit saying: "they sow smiles and laughter but shall harvest tears", and orders his Muslim office bearers that for the repairs of the temples and necessary constructions afresh they should provide cash and provisions as well as things needed for worship.
(*Maarif,* February 1918.)

Syed Sulaiman Nadvi of late lamented memory, in his article (printed in *Maarif,* February, 1918) writes : "It is alleged that Haider Ali and Tipu Sultan got Hindus circumcised forcibly and converted them to Islam. But the author of "*The Preaching of Islam,*" Mr. Arnold refutes this allegation against these two Muslim rulers' forcible conversion of Hindus to Islam in these words : "These monarchs, Haider Ali and Tipu Sultan, not far removed from our own times, have earned renown in their forcible conversion of many Hindu families and whole sections of Hindu subjects to Islam, whereas the conversion of these Hindus is an incident of much earlier period about which we know very little".

"During my journey of Madras this fact came to light. There my friends related to me that many Hindu castes of South India, particularly those of the coastal areas mostly go naked (regarding the act of vestment or clothing) an irreligious practice. Even today they have not changed their habits and customs, and the men, women and children appear frequently in their total nudity. The

Sultan had ordered them to cover their nakednes. And these orders were executed with strictness. Due to their ignorance they took as opression and tyranny this simple operation of civilizing (clothing) equivalent to conversion of Islam, when it had nothing to do with it".

THE ROLE OF MUSLIM ULAMA

As trustees and standard bearers of Islam, the Ulama have been endeavouring in every period to lighten the reins of Muslim rulers if at all they came down to do as they were pleased, and openly declaring the truth before them, they have been doing their utmost to keep them on the right track. In the Islamic teachings fearlessly delcaring the truth in the face of Jehad or fighting in the way of Allah. And it is the greatest achievement of Muslim Ulama that they have been discharging this onerous duty even at the risk of their own lives. The fact is that in the Muslim community only such daring and truth-loving Ulama have enjoyed respect and trust of the community who suffered unbearable chastisements at the hands of their Muslim rulers and regarded attachment to their courts as unbecoming to their position as learned men and pillars of the faith as also the torch bearers of its teachings (the Quran and Sunnah). From Imam Malik and Iman Abu Haneefah to Mujaddid Alf-e-Thani and Shah Wali Ullah there is a long and magnificent chain of such Ulama with temerity who dared every risk to their lives, property and honour in the discharge of their highest duty and put up with every trouble cheerfully.

What opinion these Ulama held about the style of governance and purpose of rule, a correct idea of it can be had from the writings of Shah Wali Ullah. He has written in most unambiguous terms that :

1. The real basis of wealth is labour. The labourers and cultivators are the earners of wealth and the greatest source of it. Mutual cooperation is the living spirit of culture. So long as a person does not work for the country he can have no claim to the country's wealth.[1]

2. The centres of gambling, speculation and luxury and debauchery must be closed down. In their presence the system of division of wealth in proper form cannot be established. And without boosting of production and increase in national sources of income, the wealth coming out of many pockets accumulates at one centre.[2]

3. Manual labourers cultivators and those engaged in mental toil are the real deserving recipients of the national wealth. Their progress and prospering is the progress and prosperity of the country itself. The system of government that suppresses them is a source of great danger for the country. It must end.[3]

4. The society that does not pay justly and liberally for labour put in by the wage-earner and the cultivator and taxes them heavily is an enemy of the nation and must be put to an end.[4]

---

1. For greater details please see *A Glance at the Relations of the Muslim Monarchs, Ulama and Mashaikh* by Syed Sabahuddin Abdur Rahman of Late Lamented memory.

2. See *Hujjatullah-il-Balighah*, Bab Siyasat-ul-Madaniyat, *Al Budoor-ul-Bazighah*, Mabhatul Irtifaq, *Al Khair-ul-Kathreer*.

3. *Hujjatullah-il- Balighalr Bab Iblighair - Rizq*

4. Ibid.

5. The needy on the verge of starvation consenting to the beggarly wages (offered by the hard-hearted stingly, exploiting employer) is no critierion of justice and fair play. It is fair and agreable only when he is paid the wages of his labour on the principle of mutual help. It is illgeal to exploit the starving labourer at the extremely selfish and niggardly employer's terms.[5]

6. The production of the factory and produce of the field or income, is illegal unless it is on the principle of mutual help.[6]

7. The working hours should be reduced and limited. The labourers must get enough time from their labour to look after their moral and spiritual reform and they may be able to create in themselves the capacity to think over and plan their future.[7]

8. The major means of mutual help in trade. There fore it must continue on the principle of cooperation. So just as it cannot be permitted to the traders to damage the spirit of cooperation through black-marketing or unhealthy competition, it does not behave the government either to create obstacles in the development and progress of trade.[8]

9. The business which confines the circulation of wealth to a particular class of society is ruinous for the country.[9]

---

5.   *Hujjatullah-il-Balighah*, Bab-Al-Siyasat-ul-Madaniyah, Bab Ar-Rusumus-Sairah Bain-an-Nas.

6.   *Ibid. Bablbhighair - Rizq*

7. Ibid.

8. *Hujjatullah-il-Balighah*, Bab Irtifaq, Ar-Rabi wa Bab-ul-Buyu-un-Nahi anha

9. *Hujjatullah-il-Balighah*, Babur-Rusum us Sairah Banan-Nas, wa Bab Siyasatul Madaniyah wan Bab Ibtighair-Rizq, wa Bab-ul-Buy ul manhiya.

10. That royal order of living in which due to the luxurious and wasteful style of a few individuals or families, the division of wealth is disturbed, deserves to be exterminated as early as possible so that the misery of common people may come to an end, and they may be provided a system of living on the basis of equality.[10]

11. The de facto owner of land is Allah and (according to apparent arrangement - vicegerency of man) the Islamic state. The position of the citizens of the state can be likened to those staying in an inn. His ownership means only this much that in the sphere of his utilisation and benefiting by it, no other person can interfere.[11]

12. Human beings are all equal as members of the species, And nobody has any right to regard himself or have him called Malik-e-mulk (owner of the country, Malik annas (king of mankind), Malik-e-Qaum (Lord of the people or owner of their necks). It is not becoming to any one to use such words for any one else either, in authority and rule.[12]

13. The position of a person ruling over or running a state is that of a mutawalli (a trustee of a waqf or trust). If he is needy, having no other means of livelihood of his own, he is permitted to draw from the public exchequer just enough to do existence like a common citizen of the country.[13]

---

10. Ibid
11. Ibid.
12.   Hujjatullah-il-Balighah, Bab Ibligha-ir-Rizq.
13.   Mansab-e-Imarat, Musannifah Shah Muhammed Ismail (Zikr-e-Saltanat-e-Ahallah.)

Shah Sahib (Shah Wali Ullah Mahaddith Dehlvi) has discussed in great deatil in his most famous books Hujjatullah-ul-Balighah and Al Badoor-ul-Balighah under the caption Irtifaq (Public Interest). Their sum and substance is this :

14. Enough food to subsist on in a state of sound health, enough clothing not only to cover his nakedness but to protect him from vagaries of weather and to be comfortable as also enough covered and secure room to live in comfort from the heat, cold and rain and secure from outside intervention and harm, with enough means to marry, maintain a family and look after, education and training without distinction of creed or race, is the birth right of every person.

15. Similarly without discrimination on the basis of creed, race or colour it is the fundamental right of every person to have the benefit of justice on the basis of equality in the affairs of the citizens, security of life, property, protection of their houses and dignity, freedom in the right of ownership and quality in citizenship rights.

16. To keep alive one's language and culture is the birth right of every one.

Shah Ismail Shaheed was one who regarded the kingdoms of Muslim rulers as faint and feeble state. He used to say that to pull them out root and branch is administration in the real sense and to annihilate them is Islam in its true form. To obey indiscriminately every one in authority is not the demand of the Islamic Shariah,

---

14.   Izalatul-Khifa, Vol. II Ahd-e-Faruq-e-Azam.

nor bowing down to every tyrant and usurper is the ordainment of faith. (For greater details see Mansab-e-Imamat.)

However, the Ulama to protect the country from breach of peace and anarchy, put up with these kings to some extent but lost no opportunity of conveying to and instructing them in dispensation of justice.

Hazrat Sharfuddin Yahya Maneri (Allah have Mercy on him) instructing Firoz Shah Tughlaq to be just and equitous in his dealings with the subjects, had written to him that "whoever does not listen to the cry and wailing of the oppressed will be laible to hundred cuts of a flog of fire in his grave."

Abdul Quddus Gangohi wrote to Sikandar Lodi, "justice and fairplay of a brief span are better than devotional acts of sixty years. He also quoted the tradition of the Prophet that on Doomsday the most desirable person in the sight of Allah will be a just Imam (ruler) since this beneficence of his justice was for the entire population under the care." - (*Hidustan ke Salatin, Ulama aur Mashaikh ke Taalluqat par ek Nazar*).

And this instruction and teaching was for all the citizens. If these Ulama witnessed any oppression against any non-Muslim they regarded it as their duty to raise their voice against it. They never flinched in their duty of bringing out the just ordainments of Islam in such matters.

History has preserved the record of this fact for

us that the Othmani Caliph Sultan Saleem I had a notion at one stage that to increase the number of Muslims in his empire, he should have Christian converted to Islam forcibly. But the religious leader and his advisor, Shakhul Islam Mufti Afandi opposed it vehemently and refused to issue a verdict to this effect.

The incident of the days of Lodi rulers also throws sufficient light on this trend of thought. During Sikandar Lodi's regime Hindus used to gather in large numbers at the tank of Kishtar and take bath in it. Sikandar wanted to destroy this tank and stop this gathering. He put up a query to Maulana Abdullah of his time who said in reply to it that to put a stop to an old (time-honoured) ceremony and to demolish an old seat of idol worship is not permissible under Islam. Sikandar did not relish this verdict of Maulana Abdullah and he dubbed it as partial. He also showed his temper in this unpleasantness. But the Maulana declared with great courage and without any ambiguity that he had brought out the ordainment of the Shariah in this behalf and if he heeded the Shariah so little where was the need of involving him in it.

The Ulama and mystics were ever ready for the redressal of the grievances of the oppressed and the afflicted and to control and comfort them. They detested prejudice and narrow-mindedness and kept propagating the message of tolerance and love.

After the British domination of India, in the struggle against them, the Ulama were not only in the forefront but also raised the slogans of *Muttahidah Hindustani Qaumiyat* (United Indian nationality) under

the leadership of Maulana Abul Kalam Azad who appears
most outstanding among the Ulama of the recent past.
The Ulama remained the standard bearers of Hindu
Muslim Unity. They launched a full-pledged struggle
against narrow- mindness and communalism. Apparently
they regarded it as their duty in the light of Islamic
teachings.

PART
II

BY

ALLAMA YUSUF ALQARZAWI

FIRST CHAPTER
THE RIGHTS OF NON MUSLIMS

Islamic Society is based on a particular ideology and from this fountain head emerge its ordainments, manners and morals and characters. The ideology is Islam itself. An Islamic society in the society which in its way and style of life, its constitution, the source of legislation has accepted Islam as the guide of its life in entirely all the individual, collective, temporal and spiritual, regional and international affairs.

The society does not want to get rid of other faiths in its sphere of influence but establishes firm relations between Muslims and non-Muslim citizens on the basis of goodness, benevolence, justice and tolerance. These noble bases humanity never knew before the advent of Islam (its last and most perfect version in Arabia) nor ever after during the long voyage of centuries to this day. In the modern social orders too this is sad & lacking. Sanguine struggles on the basis of religion, race and colour and prejudice, narrow mindedness, love of self and selfishness are the order of the day. Humanity is a prey to all sorts of troubles and applications.

Islam has laid down the basis of relationship with the non-Muslim on goodness and justice. And it is uniform for all those non-Muslims living in any part of the world with the Muslim in their society. The non-Muslims living in Darul-Islam or the Muslim countries,

93

they have been awarded a specific status and rights and privileges. In the Islamic terminology they are called Zimmas or Ahle-Zimmia-those living under a covenant with the Muslims and an assurance from Allah and His apostle.

The first principle in dealing with the Zimmis is that with few exceptions they enjoy the same rights and privileges that the Muslims have been granted. And so their responsibilities too are the same.

Among these rights the first is that they have the assurance of protection and support of the Islamic state and the Islamic society which includes every aggression from outside and every oppression and tyranny within, so that they may live on a stable basis in perfect peace and tranquillity.

Protection from the outside aggression is their right in the same way as that the Muslims. Imam or whoever manages the affairs of Muslims on the basis of status and military right it is binding on him to provide the Zimmis this protection. The well known book of Hambali school of jurisprudence, "*Matalib-e-ulin Nuha*" says :

It is the duty of imam to protect the zimmis. He should eliminate the source giving them trouble. If they are incarcerated he should manage their release and whoever intends to harm them should be pushed back no matter if there is any one zimmi in the entire country. Since the ordainment about zimmis have been enforced and the pact with them has an abiding value. So like Muslims their rights are also obligatory.

-*Matalib-e-ulin-Nuha*, vol. II, p. 602-603

Imam Qarani Maliki in his book "*Al Farooq*" cites the saying of Imam Ibn-e-Hazam Zahiri from his book "*Maratib-ul-Ijma*".

"If those at war with us, Muslims catch hold of some zimmi and bring him to our country, it will be binding on us to come out and give them a fight with our full might and for the protection of the life of that zimmi, who has been offered protection by Allah and his Apostle, we should lay down our own lives since without that much action, allowing them to do with the zimmis what they like shall be regarded shirking in the proper discharge of our duty. And the Ummah is one on this issue".

-Al Farooq Vol. III, p.14-15.

Allamah Qarani commenting on it has written that to save a pact from being washed, life and property may be sacrificed, is certainly very important.

As a bright example of this principle being put into action, we come upon Ibn-e-Taimiyah : when Syria came under the domination of Tartars and they had occupied it, Shaikhul-Islam went to their commander, Qatlu Shah, for the release of the prisoners of war, Qatlu Shah assented to the release of Muslim prisoners, but release of zimmis he refused. Shaikh-ul-Islam said that they could not allow Jewish and Christian prisoners to remain prisoners since they were under the protection and as such their responsibility. "We cannot leave behind any prisoner,

Muslim or non-Muslim". Qatlu Shah in view of the stern attitude of Ibn Taimiyah, set free all of them.

PROTECTION FROM INTERNAL OPPRE - SSION AND TYRANNY

Protection of zimmis from internal operation and tyranny Islam has declared compulsory, and has been very strict in the enforcement of its obligation. It warns the believers that they should in no manner try to lay hands on them, nor hurt them with the word of mouth that is disagreeable since Allah neither likes tyrants nor guides them is the right path. He inflicts punishment on them here and in the Hereafter it will be several times more severe.

Prohibition of oppression and its evil consequences in this world and the next have been emphasized in so many verses of Quran and traditions of the Prophet. And there are those also that exclusively mention the oppression and tyranny in case of non-Muslims living with Muslims under a pact. The Prophet says : "Whoever oppressed a zimmi or Muahid or deprived him of any of his rights and forced him to greater toil than he can easily undertake, or took away something from him without his willing pertain with it, I shall stand up to advocate his case on doing.

-Abu Daood, Baihaqi, As-Sumenul Kubra, Vol. V. P. 205.

In another tradition it has been said :

Whoever hurts a zimmi, I shall be the complainant against him. And my being complainant means that I shall sue him at the court.—Reported by Al Khalil.

There is yet another tradition saying :

Whoever hurts a zimmi hurts me. And whoever hurts me hurts Allah. - Tabrani, Fil Ausat.

That is why right from the time of the rightly guided caliphs the believers have been very attentive and careful in preventing oppression and tyranny to zimmis in any form, saving them from every trouble that could come their way, investigating every matter thoroughly in which they happened to put up a complaint.

Umer, the second rightly guided caliph tried to find out the condition of zimmis, in particular from all those delegations coming from different parts of the Islkamic state, lest thay may come by some harm. And these delegates hold him that to the best of their knowledge Zimmis were being treated justly, according to the terms of the pact, meaning that the Muslims were fulfilling what was due from them to the zimmis - both parties cooperating.

-Tarikh-e-Tabri, Vol. IV. P. 218.

Ali, the fourth rightly guided caliph used to say :

They pay Jizyah so that their lives and properties may become prohibited like ours.

Al Mughni, Vol. VIII, P. 445, *Al Badai* Vol. VII, P. 111

All the Mujtahid Fuqaha (The erudite among the jurists) of all the Juristic Schools have clearly stated in the decisive way that this is an obligation of the Muslims that they should protect the zimmis from all sorts of oppression and tyranny. And after the covenant between them their status becomes the same (with few exceptions), as that of Muslims. Rather, some jurists have gone to the extent in their opinions in this behalf that the oppression and tyranny in case of a zimmi shall be deemed more serious than that perpetrated on the Muslim. For example Ibm Abideen in a marginal note of his says that since a zimmi in Darul Islam regards himself weaker than the Muslim, oppression of the strong on the weak shall be deemed more serious in nature.

The apostle of Allah has said :

Whoever murders a zimmi shall remain deprived of the preagrance of paradise when it can be enjoyed at a distance of (that could be covered in) forty years.

-Ahmad, Bukhari, Nasai, Abu Daood and Tirmaizi reported by Ali.

Imam Abu Haneefah, Imam Shabi, Imam Nakhai, Ibn-e-Abi Lalia, Ullman-al-Nabi and the disciples of Abu Haneefah are all of the opinion that for the murder of a zimmi, a believer will pay with his life, since the Book of Allah and the Sunnah of the Prophet are firm on Qisas as the general rule here and the prohibition of shedding blood as an abiding law. Also it is reported from the Prophet that he had a Muslim killed for the murder of a zimmi, and had remarked, "who can have greater regard for pact than I."   - Abdur Razzaq, Baihaqui.

Moreover there is a report from Ali that a Muslim was brought to him who had murdered a zimmi, and it had been conclusively proved also. He ordered that the

(Muslim) murderred should be put to death. The brother of the murdered came to him (Ali) and said that he had forgiven the murderer. Ali said to him that probably the relative of the murderred had threatened him. He said, no. Nothing like that. The fact is that by taking his life he could not get back his brother. And over and above that they have also paid him the recompense for it. Ali said to him, "you understand your own affairs better. But whatever lies in our power is that the quality of his blood is like that of ours and his <u>diyat</u> (blood money) is also like ours".
-Tabrani, Baihaqi

In another report Ali is reported to have said, "they paid Jizyah so that the sanctity of their lives and property may become like those of ours".

Umar bin Abdul Aziz reports that he ordered one of his governors about a person who had murdered a zimmi that he (the murderer) should be handed over to the patron of the zimmi. He may take his life if he is inclined that way or he may forgive him. So that murderer was entrusted to the care of the patron of the murdered, and he (the patron) killed him with one stroke of his sword.
-Musannif Abdur Razzaq

The jurists assert that it is on this basis of equality that the person stealing the goods of a zimmi forfeits his hand to the Islamic Shariah, since property is less important than life.

As for the Prophet's edict that no Muslim shall be killed for a non-Muslim," alludes to a non-Muslim at war with Muslims. See *Ahkam-ul-Quran* by Imam Jassas,
Vol. I. P. 140-144.

It was this Sumrah or way that Uthmani Caliphate enforced and acted upon in the regions under its control, until through the untiring efforts of the enemies of Islam it came to a tragic end.

It is not only that Islam has provided protection to the lives of the zimmis but has also given surety of protection from any physical hurt. Even if they delay payment of Jizyah and Khiraj (land revenue) they cannot be liable to corporal punishment, whereas if the Muslims were to delay payment of zakat, they will be dealt with harshly. The jurists have left room in taking to back the zimmis for shopping payment of government dues, that they should be incarcerated as a corrective measure but without any punishment or taking any work from them involving labour. Imam Abu Yusuf has written that a companion of the Prophet Hakeem Bin Hisham witnessed that the ruler of Hams was chastising the defaulters in payment of Jizyah, by making them stand forcibly in the scorching heat of the sun, asked what was the matter, "I have heard the Prophet saying", said he, "that those who oppress people here in this world, Allah shall make out punishment to them in the Hereafter"
Muslim.

-See <u>Kitab-ul-Khiraj</u>, p. 125 and Sunan-e-Baihaqi Vol. IV, p. 205.

Ali the fourth rightly guided caliph instructed one of his revenue officers in writing : "When you get to them (for collection of Jizyah) don't (in your zeal) sell their clothes and their food articles, nor the animals that meet their needs. Do not so much as give any of them even one out of your whip, nor make them stand on their feet (by way of punishment) for realization of dues, nor sell any of their goods for Khiraj. For, we have been ordered to take from their surplus goods only. If you disobey these instructions Allah will hold you responsible for that irregularity before I am questioned about it. And if the information about these irregularities on your part finds its way to me, I will dismiss you from your post". The revenue officer said to him, "With those conditions of restraint I shall come back to you empty handed as I am leaving". The caliph, Ali retorted, "Even if you return empty handed".

-Kitabul Khiraj, p. 15-16, Sunan-e-Baihaqi,
Vol. IX, p. 205.

Like the protection of life and limb, that of property has also been given. There has been consensus of Muslims on it in every period, region and of every school of juristic order.

Imam Abu Yusuf has narrated an incident of the period of the Prophet, relating to the people of Najran, that he had assured them of the protection from Allah. His Apostle, about their property, their religion, their deals of sale and purchase and whatever is in their possession. -Kitab-ul-Khiraj, p. 72

During the period of Umar Farooq, the Commander in Chief Abu Ubaidah bin-ul-Jarah was sent instruction to the effect that Muslims should not be allowed to oppress the zimmis, hurt them in any way and taking away their property illegally, should never be permitted.

Ali's saying has just been quoted above that the zimmis have paid Jizyah only to make sure that their lives and properties also become immune like those of Muslims. And the Muslims have to abide by this principle. So if any one stole the property of a zimmi, his hand was chopped off. And one who usurped the property of any one among the zimmis he was punished and the usurped property restored to the owner. And whoever borrowed from a zimmi, he had to return it to him. And if the debtor was not a bankrupt and could pay back the loan, dilly dallying due to mischief, the Qazi shall cast him into jail for his misbehaviour, until he returns the debt.

Islam cared so much for the protection of the zimmi's property that they respected even that which according to Muslims is not property at all, such as wine and pigs. If these things are in possession of a Muslim and somebody destroys them, there is neither any penalty for it nor punishment. Rather, he will be deemed worthy of the reward in the Hereafter. For, Muslims are strictly prohibited from keeping these things with them, neither for themselves nor with intention of selling them.

But these commodities, wine and pigs, if they are in possession of the non-Muslim, they will be regarded as his property. Rather, according to the jurists of the Hanafite school, it will be declared their valuable property. And any one destroying this property shall have to pay the entire cost in the form of fine.

PROTECTION OF HONOUR AND DIGNITY

Islam ensures the protection of honour and dignity of the zimmis with the same care with which the honour and dignity of the Muslims are protected. No one can be permitted to reproach a zimmi or bring a false accusation against him, or attribute things to him that are false, back-bite him, or say things about his personality, his lineage, physical condition, habits and morals that may not be agreeable to him. Malikite jurist Shahabuddin Qarafi writes :

"The pact of Zimmah makes us liable to the responsibilities concerning the rights of the zimmis, since they are with us and under our protection as also the super-protection provided by Allah, his Apostle and Islam

-*Al Farooq*, Vol. III, P. 14.

The well known book of Hanafites School, *Durr-e-Mukhtar* says :

To remove the trouble or injury from a zimmi is a Muslims obligation and back-biting him is strictly prohibited as 'it is in case of a Muslim.

Allamah Ibn Abideen commenting on it writes :

This is for the reason that along with the pact of responsibility, the rights of a zimmi became the same as ours. So if back-biting a Muslim is prohibited it is the same in case of a zimmi. Rather it is said that injury to a zimmi is of a more serious nature.

-See Durr-e-Mukhtar, Marginal Notes by Ibn Abideen Vol. III. p. 344-346.

And above all these rights and privileges, Islam in its tributaries provides surety of useful employment and earning their livelihood for the non-Muslims, since they are also subjects of the Islamic state and for this reason are answerable for all its subjects without distinction. The Apostle of Allah says : "Every one of your supervisors is responsible for all those placed under his charge".

-Unanimous, reported by Ibn Umar

During the period of the rightly guided caliphs and even after them, this has been the practice of the Islamic state. Khalid bin Waleed had also written in the pact with the zimmis, the citizens of Heerah in Iraq that whenever anyone of them becomes too old to work for his livelihood or that he falls a prey to some disability or calamity or becomes a pauper from a position of prosperity and his debtors start giving him alms, the levy of Jizyah shall be terminated, and he and his family shall be supported by the Muslim Bait-ul-Mal (Public Exchequer). *-Kitab-ul-Khiraj*, p. 144.

This incident referred to above briefly, belongs to the period of Abu Bakr and a large number of the companions were witness to it. Khalid Bin Waleed wrote about it to Abu Bakr and nobody differed in his opinion on it. Such a process is declared Ijma (consensus).

Umar Farooq saw an old man extending his open hand before the way-farers and asked about him, (the old and decrepit beggar). He was told that his extremely old age and dire need have compelled him to beg. He took that beggar with him to the Baitul Mal and instructed the person in charge to give him and other indigent persons like him, at least enough to restore them to a status of meeting their needs without begging. He had also added that realizing Jizyah from him in his youth and when old and totally disabled, leave him to debase himself (with begging) would be a grave injustice.

Umar, when he was passing through Jabiyah in Syria noticed some Christian lepers. At once he ordered that they should be given a lump sum from the fund of Sadaqat and they should also receive their daily dole, which means that the state should undertake to feed them free of charge. - *Futuh-ul-Buldan*, Al-Balazari, P. 177

In this way Social insurance was acknowledged as a principle which covers all the citizens of the state irrespective of their religion. In this way there was no justification left for leaving out any one hungry, naked or without a roof over his head, since removing trouble or hardship from every citizen is a religious obligation, he may be a Muslim or a zimmi.

Allamah Shamsuddin Ramali Shafii has written in his book, "*Nihayatul Muhtaj ila-Sharahil Minhaj* that zimmis in this connection are like Muslims. So removing afflictions from them is an obligatory duty of Muslims. Proceeding further, Allamah while discussing other ways of removing afflictions, writes as to what is actually meant by it - giving just enough to keep the body and soul together or to meet their entire satisfaction. The more correct opinion is that the afflicted persons should get enough to feed and clothe himself properly. This includes the restments of the hot and cold weather. Also the fees of a doctor, cost of medicines (in sickness) and the services of a helper (conventionally called servant) should also be included.

Similarly, obtaining the release of Muslims and zimmis is a part of removing affliction.

-See Nihayatul Muhtaj, ilash-Sharah-il-Minhaj Lil Ramali, Vol. VIII, P. 46.

RELIGIOUS FREEDOM

The rights of zimmis which have been assured to them, freedom is also one of them. And the most important freedom is that of creed and worship. Every one has his religion and creed. He can neither be forced to change it, nor for leaving it and accepting Islam not any pressure can be brought to bear on him. It is based on the divine injunction.

There is no compulsion in religion. Truth stands out clear from Error. (Q. II : 256)

And, Wilt than compel mankind, against his will, to believe   Al Quran X : 99

Ibn-e-Katheer writes while commenting on the just of these two Quranic verses : Nobody should be compelled to enter the fold of Islam, since it is clear enough and its very bright arguments do not stand in need of force to make them acceptable. Ibn Abbas reports that during the period of Jahiliyah (ignorance or Un-Islam), it was a custom that if an Ansari woman was issueless or with one or two issues only, the husband and wife would take a vow that if any of their male progeny survived they would have him converted to Judaism. When Banu Nadheer were exiled from Madinah there were several Ansari boys along with them. Their fathers asserted that they would not let their sons go with the exiled Jews (meaning that they would not let them remain Jews so that they may also be exiled). Then Allah revealed this verse.

Other traditionalists have also cited reports like this about the reason and occasion of its revelation.

-See *Tafseer Ibn Katheer*, Vol. I, P. 310.

In spite of the fact that the emphasis on compulson was from the fathers of the converts to Judaism who wanted to save their sons from the enemies of their religion and race, and in spite of the peculiar condition under which those sons of theirs at an early age had been made Jews, and in spite of the fact that with at period those opposing religion and cult were mercilessly oppressed (as it had happened in the Russian empire that the people there were given the choice of either getting converted to Christianity or get killed. Then, with the change in the religion of the state to "Malakani", those opposing it, Jacobites and other sects of christianity were mercilessly massacred). In spite of all that the Quran turned down compulsion in religion. Whomsoever Allah guides to the right path opens his breast for receiving this guidance, he may embrace Islam with the entire satisfaction of his heart. And one in whose heart this divine light cannot peneterate what use is there in the formality of converting him to Islam, since in the words of Ibn Katheer belief is not, according to the Muslims just utterance of Kalimah and performance of some ceremonies physically. Its basis is on the affirmation, belief and submission from the depth of the converted person's heart.

That is why we do not come upon any example in history where a Muslim might have compelled zimmis to accept Islam. This fact has been acknowledged by the historians of the west too.

Similarly, Islam has given surety of the protection of their places of worship and also the sanctity of their customs and manners. Rather, the Quran has also included among causes of permission of waging war for the protection of the freedom of worship :

To those against whom war is made, permission is given (to fight) because they are wronged - and verily Allah is the Most Powerful for their aid,

(They are) Those who have expelled from their homes in difference of right, - (for no cause) except that they say "Our Lord is Allah". Did not Allah check one set of people by means of another, there would surely have been pulled down monasteries, churches, synagogues and mosques, in which the name of Allah is commemorated in abundant measure.   -Al-Quran XXII : 39:40

We have seen earlier how during the period of the Prophet, the people of Najran were provided surety in matters relating to the freedom of their religion, and property and it was declared surety from Allah and His Apostle.

During the period of Umar Bin Khattab the pact with the citizens of Eliah (Quds) was concluded in these words:

The servant of Allah, Amir-ul-Mumineen (the commander of the faithful) offered amensty to the citizens of Eliah, surety of their lives and properties, the protection of their churches and crosses and their faith. No one is going to meddle with their churches, nor demolish or damage them, nor their cross be snatched from them, nor yet any of their property shall be taken away from them, nor any pressure brought to bear on them regarding their religion, none of them shall be given any trouble, nor shall any Jew stay with them in Eliah.

-Tarikh Tabri, Vol. III, P. 608

The pact that Khalid bin Waleed entered with the residents of Anat had this sentence included in its subject matter : "Barring the fixed hours of prayers they can sound their conch shells whenever they like and during the days of their jubilation and festivities they can have their crosses taken around on public roads freely.

-Kitab-ul-Khiraj P. 146

Islam demands of the non-Muslims that they should have some regard for the feelings of Muslims and should not trample the sanctity of their faith. They should not put up a demonstration in some Muslim locality which might injure the feelings of the Muslims and kick up tumult and disturbances.

Many of the jurists have permitted construction of their places of worship by the zimmis. In those lands which have been subdued after sanguine battles and the people there have surrendered after long severe resistance, those too the ruler has the right to permit the non-Muslims to build their places of worship. Freedom of the Preachers of their creed is ensured any way.

This is the opinon of Zaidis and Imam Ibn Qayim

-See <u>Ahkamul Zimmieen and Mustamineen</u>, P. 96-99

The history of Muslims tells us that it is in practice from the very beginning. In the first century of the Muslim calendar(Hijrah) many churches were built in Egypt. The famous church of Alexandria 'Marmaqas' was build between 39 and 56 A.H. The first church of Fustat was built during the governership of Muslimah bin Mukhallad between 47 and 68 A.H., when Halwan city was built and inhabited by Abdul Aziz bin Merwan he also permitted the construction of a church. Similarly, they, the clergymen were allowed to construct two monasteries. Many such examples have come for mention in Maqreezi's book '*Al-khilafat*', and concluding his remarks he has said that all the churches of Cairo were built during the period of the Islamic rule.

-See Dr. Ali Hasan Kharbotali's book of '*Islam aur Ahle-Zimmah*', P. 129 and that by Thomas Arnold *Dawat-e-Islam* (Preaching of Islam), Arabic translation P. 84-86.

As for those villages and lands that are not regarded as Muslim areas, there they are perfectly free to have demonst- rations of their customs and manners any time they like. (There is no one to interfere or put any checks on their social and religious activities).

From such a people whose life rests entirely on their faith, and through faith they came to success and domination also, toleration of this degree for the opponents of their faith, is a rare example, not met anywhere in the history of religion. The westerners have themselves acknowledged this fact.

The famous French author, Gustav Labon writes :

The Quranic verses we have just mentioned, tell us that the tolerance of Muhammad Sal'am with the Jews and Christians was of a very high order. No such thing is traceable in the founders of the religions before him, particularly Judaism and Christianity. We find his caliphs following his Sunnah (way). This tolerance has been acknowledged by the most sceplic learned men of Europe, as also those who have studied minutely the history of the Arabia. The quotations taken from many of their books go to prove that we are not alone in having this view about. him. For example in his book 'History of Sharikin' Rebertson writes that the Muslims are the only people that along with the highest regard for the dignity of their own faith, they combined tolerance for the followers of other religions. And though they were very enthusiastic in propagating their own religion, those who had no liking for Islam, they left alone, free to stick firmly to and practise their own religion.

> -Marginal note of Arabian Culture, translated by Adil, P. 128.

FREEDOM OF EARNING LIVELIHOOD

Islam provides surety of the freedom of earning their livelihood to non-Muslims. They are at liberty to undertake any business independently or in partnership with Muslims. They may take to any of the professions they like and like Muslim may participate in any economic activity they are pleased.

The jurists are of the opinion that in sale and purchase, trade and financial matters, zimmis and Muslims are on an equal footing. And the business involving interest is no exemption for them strictly prohibited to both equally. The Apostle of Allah had witten to Maqii of Hijr to either abandon business with interest or become prepared to face the opposition of Allah and His Apostle.

Similarly zimmis will not be allowed to sell wine and pigs in Muslim settlements. Public bars and pubs and advertisements of wine shall be strictly prohibited. And these measures have been adopted to close the doors in evils and corruptions raising their head in society. The Muslims are reallly bound by these limits.

Barring these few items, zimmis enjoyed perfect freedom in industry and trade. And this has also been the practice in the Islamic world. The history of Muslims in various periods has borne testimony to it. Rather, the financial dealings which in modern terminology are called banking and medical practice and pharmacy have been the monopoly of the zimmi non-Muslims and in most Muslim countries till the recent past this monopoly had contained and persists to this day in some degree. With these proferrious solely in their domain the non-Muslims have been amassing enormous wealth, when barring a nominal poll tax, Jizyah, they are exempt not only from Zakat but have no other tax to pay that Muslim are bound to pay. The jizyah too was so small an amount and levied only on able bodied combatfit men, women, children, old and disabled and decrepit persons and ascelics enjoying exemption.

Adam Metz writes :

"There was nothing in the Islamic Shariah which could close the doors on any works that the zimmis could undertake. In the most profitable industries their feet were firmly fixed. In medical practice, preparation and sale of drugs land perfumes as also in trade and feudalism they held a position of monopoly. Rather, the zimmis had organized themselves in such a manner that most of those dealing in money matters in Syrai were Jews, and medical men and those looking after the executive and the secreteriate mostly Chiristians. In Baghdad the leader of the Christians was the physician attending on the caliph, and a large number of outstanding Jews were constantly in attendance on him.

-See Islamic culture in the fourth century after Hijrah, Arabic translation, Vol. I P. 86

The posts which a religious stamp on them, for example Imamat (leadership both spiritual and temporal) the job of heading the Islamic state (conducting the affairs of the state and matters of policy of an Islamic state), the supreme command of the fighting forces, the Qazis entrusted with the job of settling disputes of Muslims and the supervision of the realization of zakat and sadaqat. With these few exceptions appointments to all other posts were open to Muslim and non-Muslims alike.

The position of imarat (leadership) and caliphate (succession by general consent in authority and rule) in Islam has both sides, temporal and spiritual. So no non-Muslim could get appointed to it, since only a Muslim, well versed in the Islamic Shariah could conduct its afairs efficiently. Similarly, the supreme command of the mies was not regarded as a solear job, but a deveotional act of great importance in the Islamic order.

Similarly, Qaza means deciding disputes according to the dictates of the Islamic Shariah. And one who did not believe in the Islamic law itself. And one who did not believe in the Islamic law itself, obviously enough could not be expected to discharge this duty (apart from efficiency or lack of it). The supervision of the collection of zakat and other sadaqat (charities) were also religious in nature.

Leaving alone these few jobs of religious importance all others were available to zimmis conditional to capability and loyalty to the Islamic state, honesty and integrity. They should not always be bent on hostility to Muslims. Apparently in keeping with the capability, integrity and loyalty in keeping with the importance of the post are regarded essential conditions for service in every society. It is this fact that the Quran has alluded to in the following verse :

Oye who believe : Take not into your intimacy those outside your ranks : they will not fail to corrupt you. They only desire your ruin : Rank hatred has already appeared from their mouths : what their hearts conceal is far worse. We have

made plain to you the sign; if you have wisdom.
-Al Quran III. P. 118

Toleration extended and touched those limits that jurists like Mawardi wrote clearly that a zimmi can be entrusted with the ministry of enforcement (ordainments, laws, principles and rules and regulations). This post was burdened with the responsibility of enforcing the command of the imam and the caliphate and have them put into practice, just in the same way as there was a post in the Islamic set up of ministy of Tafweez - the imam and the caliph used to assign the responsibility of the supervision of political economic affairs to a minister.

During the Abbasid dynasty, the ministry of Tanfeez (implementation) was entrusted to a christian. Nasr bin Haroon in 369 A.H. and Isa bin Nastur as in 380 A.H. Muawiyah himself had a christian secretary, Sarjon by name.

In this behalf the toleration of Muslims attained heights where the rights of Muslims were trampled and they were found complaining against the appointments of incapable zimmis to posts of responsibility.

Adam Metz writes :

"The matters which astonish us one of them is the plethora of non-Muslim office bearers and senior officers, in the Islamic country's set up. The reality appears to be that in the Islamic countries Muslims were grooming under the despotic rule of the Christians. The complaint of Muslims about giving the zimmis undue lift is an old one".

-Islami Tehzeeb Chauthi Sadi Hijri men
Vol. I. P. 105

An Egyptian poet Hasan bin Khaqan says :

In this period the Jews have attained their highest ambitions, glory, greatness and worldly goods are only with them. The adviser is from them and the ruler also from them. Oye Egyptian I advise you that - Become Jews, the heaven itself has become a Jew (The entire working order has been pampering Jews and Judaism). Imam Suyuti has quoted these couplets in *Husu-ul-Hazirah.*

-See Vol. II. P. 117 and Islami Tahzeb,
Adam Metz, Vol. I. P. 118.

The well-known Hanafite Jurist, Ibn Abideen, in his period noticed the preference of non-Muslims over Muslims, unitl it came to a stage where they began to decide cases relating to Ulama and jurists and other Muslim learned men. Thus moved he quoted the following couplets in his writing :

Friends : The calamities in this world are manifold. But the bitterest affliction is that of undue lift to fools. When will the people awaken from their sound slumber, where as I am witnessing here the jurists being a based and insulted by the Jews.

-Marginal note of Abideen Vol. III, P. 378

This state of affairs had been witnessed when in the period of their decline and decay the Muslim society had fallen a prey to ignorance and disruption and the Jews pervaded the scene (and dominated and oppressed them due to their abiding hostility to Islam and the Muslims).

The last evidence furnished by history is with reference to the Uthmani empire which to its last day kept appointing their (apparently faithful non-Muslim citizens to posts of great importance and delicacy. And even for the representation of the so called Islamic state in foreign countries these non-Muslims were sent out as agents and envoys.

SURETY FOR THE FULFILMENT OF THE RIGHTS

The Islamic Shariah along with conferring on the non-Muslims all these rights and freedoms, stressed on the Muslims that they should deal with them in a pleasant manner.

Even then what was the guarantee of these rights and instruction being implemented and complied with impractial life, particularly in a situation when the differences of creed could so often become an obstacle. When we look at the constitutions and laws - all man made - it is clearly visible that equality in the matter of rights between the citizens has been mentioned in most main biqulous and emphatic terms, but impractical life remain on paper. The laws cannot overcome the prejudices of people, since the common people neither regard them sacred nor at heart they believe in and agreee with them, nor yet consider compliance with them necessary. They represent the hue feelings of the populace.

SURETY BASED ON CREED

But since the Islamic Shariah is of the divine origin, and enjoys the lofliest position among the heavenly laws

(Shariahs) which can not permit any change, nor can there be any room in it for oppression or excess, nor faith and belief be perfect without obedience and submission to it with our open mind. It has been stated clearly in the Quran :

It is not fitting for a believer, man or woman, when a matter has been decided by Allah and his Apostle, to have any option about his decision. If any one disobeys Allah and His Apostle, he is indeed clearly on a wrong path. (Q. XXXIII, 36)

Therefore it is the desire of every religious minded Muslim to implement the ordainments and instructions of the Shariah so that he may expect reward of the Hereafter for it and Allah may be pleased with him.In this connection he is totally unmindful of the feelings of relationship, friendship and enmity and opposition; Allah says :

Oye who believe : stand out firmly for justice as witnesses to Allah, even as against yourselves, or your parents or your kin,   (Q. IV: 135)

Again,

Oye who believe : stand out firmly for Allah, as witness to fair dealing, and let not the hatred of others to you make you serve to wrong and depart form justice. Be just, that is next to piety : and fear Allah, for Allah is well-acquainted with all that ye do.

-Al Quran V. 9

SURETY PROVIDED BY
THE MUSLIM SOCIETY

In the same way the Muslim society is charged with the responsibility of enforcing the Shariah and apply its ordainments to all affairs of life. Ordainments pertaining to non-Muslims are also there. Now if somebody furnishes proof of his shortcoming or totally swerving from it, or is guilty of oppression and tyranny himself, there must be some people in the Muslim society who can hold his hand and ally with the oppressed even if he is a follower of some other religion.

It is possible in case of his nonchalant as well as when he comlaints of it (oppression). In the seond situation most likely there will be men to listen to his grievance and manage its redressal, no matter how powerful and influential the person against whom justice has to be done.

A zimmi will be within his rights if he complains to the local authority nearest to him and very likely he may get justice at this level. In case of failure, he has the right to complain sraight to the caliph. He must get his grievance redressed here. Even if the contention lies between him and the caliph himself there will be that free and independent judiciary to bring justice to him. He will have the right to sue the caliph if necessary. Moreover, the jurists who are also protectors and supporters of the public opinion will be sureties of his help and support to him.

Still greater guarantee is the conscience of the

Islamic world which is shaped by the Islamic creed, Islamic training and Islamic traditions.

Islamic history is replete with incidents that bear testimony to the fact that Islamic society for the protection of the rights of zimmis and their freedom has stood, against every tyranny, in their support. If a Muslim has tyrannised a zimmi, the local administrative and judicial authority, immediately on learning about it will try to take action against it and make amends to him.

A Christian friar of Egypt complained to the governor, Ahmad bin Tuluen, against a military commander that he had illegally taken some of his goods from him. Ibn Tulune immediately called the military commander and after menacing him, his snatched goods was restored to the friar, saying that if the asvetic hand shown his claim to several times more such goods he would have given it to him. Ibn Tulune had kept his door open to every oppressed zimmi, no matter what position the respondent occupied - a military commander, a high placed civil officer had no imporance to him in such matters.

And if the governor himself happens to be the oppressor any tyrant or his household or companions, it becmoes the responsibility of the caliph himself to do justice to him. Its brightest example is that incident in which the son of the governor of Egypt, Umro bin al-As, a companion, had whipped the boy of a local citizen of the coplic origin and said that he was the son of a noble person. The copt ws infuriated and got to the seat of the Islamic state at Madinah and put up his grievacne before the caliph, Umar Ibn ul Khatee. Amirul Mumineen called Umro bin al-As, the governor and his son to the capital city and handing over a lash to the copt's son said to him, "whip the son of the noble person as you have been whipped". When the boy had finished the job, Umar turning to him said, "Now turn your lash to Umro since his son had beaten you because of his father's authority and rule. The copt said, "Whoever had beaten me I am quits with him. That's enough". Then Umar Farooq turned to Umro bin-ul-As and said what is worth its letters in gold in the World History : "Umro : Since when you have made people your slaves, their mothers ahd borne them free".

In this incident a point worthy of comment is this also as to how had the common people come to have a sense of honour and self-respect under the Islamic rule, so much so that if a person received a slap unjustly, he stood up and cried for justice. Whereas in the Roman empire much more serious incidents were a common occurence and raised no protest and demand for justice. But under the blessed shade of Islam every one had come to have such a regard for self respect and rights that he would even undertake long and tedious journeys under great hardships, get to far far away Madinah, from Egypt because he was sure that he would be heard sympathetically and must get justice there.

Again, if the grievance of a zimmi could not find its way to the caliph or he too adopted the attitude of the oppressive governor, the jurists of Islam representing the Muslim public opinion and all the religious minded

Muslims were ever ready to aid and support an oppressed person.

During the Abassis period, the zimmis of Jabal Lebanon demostrated their opposition to the revenue officer collecting khiraj. The local authority or the governor of the region who happened to be a relative of the caliph and close to him (Swaleh bin Ali bin Abdullah bin Abbas), ordered exile, enmas, of the zimmis from the province. When Imam Auzai came to know of it he wrote a very menacing letter saying :

How can an entire lot of common people be made to suffer for the fault of a few defaulters, that they should be turned out of their homes and other properties when Allah has said that, No bearer of burdens shall bear the burden of mother.   (Q. XVII : 15)

The Divine Injunctions must be aced upon as a matter of utmost priority. Then the ordainments and the instruction of the Appostle of Allah are most essential. And he has said, "Whoever opposes a zimmi and casts on him a burden that he cannot bear, I shall stand to plead his cause -". He, Imam Auzai further goes on to say, "These zimmis are not slaves that you can move them from one place to another. They are free men and under our protection".

-Al Amwal le Abi Ubaid, P. 170-171

There is no example in the Islamic history that oppression and tyranny perpetrated against zimmis might have countinued for any length of time without action being take against the culprits for, public opinion, which was invariable supported by Ulama and jurists, always stood up against them and an usurped right or freedom was soon restored.

The ummayyid caliph, Waleed bin Abdul Malik took away John's Church from the christians and made it a part of the building of the mosque. After a very brief interval when Umar bin Abdul Aziz was elected caliph, the Christians complained to him about his irregularity. The caliph wote to this governor that the extended portion of the mosque be handed over to the christians.

The historian Bilazari has furnished details of this incident that right from Muawiyah to Abdul Malik, the caliphs had been trying to induce the Christians to part with that church willingly so that the pressing need of extension of the mosque be thus met. But the Christians had all along insisted on their refusal to oblige. Then Waleed during his time called together the Christians, and to purchase this piece of land he offered an enormous amount. But the Christians were adamant. Unpleasantness was created during hot exchanges and Waleed in a rage threatened them saying that if they do not surrender willingly he would be obliged to take it by force and demolished the portion of the church he needed for extension of the mosque. One of the christians said that one who demolishes churches becomes mad and a cripple. This uncivil and insulting remark further infuriated Waleed and picking up a spade he himself started the demolition. Others immediately followed suit and completed the job. And his portion of the church became part of the mosque. When Umar bin Abdul Aziz became caliph the matter was put up before him. He wrote to his governor that portion of the mosque be demolished and the vacated piece of land be returned to the christians. The Muslims took it asserting that the portion of the mosque where they had offered prayers ought not have been demolished. Sulaiman bin Habib Maharibi and other jurists went to the Christians and said to them that the mosque (extension) has been constructed, they should give up their demand and in return for it, restoration of all their important places in the newly conquered region of ghote after a fullfledged battle, can be granted to them. Then it was referred to the caliph for his sanction and he generously assented. And thus this episode came to an happy end. -See *Fatuhul Buldan*, P. 171-172

Waleed bin Yazeed in view of the Romans (christian's) intended attack as a matter of precaution transferred the zimmis of Cyprus to Syria. It was very much disapproved by the jurists and the common people. Again, when Yazeed bin Waleed brought them back to Cyprus, the Muslims showed their happiness and credited the incident to Waleed's acts of justice.

-Futuhul Buldan, P. 114.

A great asset of the Islamic order is its judicial order. In this system every oppressed, no matter to which religion and sex the person belongs, justice is guaranteed. This system is surety for bringing to justice anyone however strong and high placed like the Amir of the believers and force him to restore to the oppressed whatever he had been deprived of. In the history of the Islamic order of justice there are many incidents when the caliph or Sultan (the ruler) has to appear before the court as seeker of justice or a respondent in case of injustice to any one, and in most cases the case was decided in favour of a weak, helpless person. Here we are presenting just one example. Ali Ibn Abi Talib dropped his coat of mail somewhere. He saw it in the possession of a christion. Both went to Qazi Shuraih seeking justice. Ali asserted that the coat of mail was his and he had neither sold it nor given it to anybody. When the Qazi questioned the christian as to what he had to say. He claimed its rightful possession, still he believed Amirul Mumineen could not tell lies. Qazi Shuraih asked Ali if he had any proof of his claim. Ali smiled, saying he had no proof to the effect. At this stage Qazi Shuraih decided the case in favour of the christian since no proof could be brought against his defacts possession. The christian left with the 'prize', but turned back on his heels with the passionate but burst that such decisions are remain out of those of the prophets. Amirul Mumineen brings me here to his Qazi who decided the case against him, then he embraced Islam and admitted, "The coat of mail belongs to you. When you were returning from the battle of Siffin, it had fallen from your camel. I was behind the army and had picked it up. Ali was very much pleased with this sudden change of heart and offered that coat of mail to him as a gift.

-Ibne Katheer

CHAPTER - II
THE RESPONSIBILITIES OF
NON-MUSLIMS

In the preceding chapter we have discussed in detail the rights and freedoms of zimmis and the guarantee of their being put into effect. Now we have to see what obligations and responsibilities they have to shoulder on the principle of reciprocity in this pact.

Under the Islamic Shariah among the financial responsibilities of zimmis, Jizyah, Khiraj and the taxes pertaining to trade are their only obligations.

Apart from that the matters which do not concern their faith, such as murder, in them like Muslims, only Muslim laws will apply. Moreover, it will be expected of them on moral grounds that they do not openly desecrate the Islamic ways, customs and manners.

JIZYAH

Jizyah[15] is an annual tax levied on ablebodied (combat-fit men who are in a position to pay it. It is a nominal amount that is easy to pay. Poor, indigent persons, women, children decrepit and disabled persons, as well as ascetics are exempted, since Allah has said :

---

15. Allamah Shibli Nomani writes about Jizyah :

Really this word Jizyah is an Arabicised form of the Persian world 'Gazeel' and was initiated by Nausherwan Adil. The historian Abu Jafar Tabri has written about the administration of Nausherwan that with various considerations he had levied Gazeel or Jizyah, as we now call ➲

"Allah puts no burden on any one beyond what he has given him.   -Al Quran XXV : 7

There is no definite amount fixed by the Shariah for Jizyah. Rather the Imam or the caliph has the right to fix the amount according to the financial position of the person without involving him in difficulties.

Umar bin-al-Khattab levied 48 dirhams on the more prosperous among the well off persons, middle income group had pay 24 dirhams, and the less prosperous only 12 dirhams annually. In this way he (Umar) is also regarded as the founder

---

⊃it, on his people. But the nobility, the elite, the army, the religious leaders and writers were exempt. Also those who were on the wrong side of fifty or less than 20 years were exempted. After the conquest of Persia. Umar Farooq continued this practice with minor corrections. It is also mentioned that Nausherwan had said : The army is the protector of the country for which they hazard their lives. Therefore a certain amount was allocated from the earnings of people in general for the fighting forces which may compensate them for the hardships and hazard to life.

According to the administrative set up of Islam even Muslims could be compelled to take up arms (conscription) for the protection and maintenance of the Islamic state. But it was not so easy. And the people if they could find an excuse wanted to take advantage of it. So once when the teachers of maktabs in Sicily were exempted from military service, people, leaving other jobs by hundreds entered this trade, to escape conscription. (*Mujim-ul-Buldan*). And since all the able bodies Muslims performed military service they were exempted form Jizyah. And the followers of other religions, because they could not be compelled to undertake military service it became necessary to make them pay some sort of tax for their protection. This amount that they were made to pay came to be called jizyah. If on some (rare) occasion they (the non-Muslims) consented to take up arms for the protection of the country, they were exempted from Jizyah - *Maqalat-e-Shibli* Vol. I., P. 231.

of levy of taxes on people, according to their financial condition (proportionate tax). The Prophet himself when he had sent Muaz to Yemen he had instructed him to realize one dirham from every major male capable of payment. Since there was lack of prosperity in Yemen, the Prophet made allowance for the people. So there was no contradiction between this and Umar's edicts.

The obligation of Jizyah is based on the following Quranic verse :

Fight those who believe not in Allah, nor the Last Day, nor hold that forbidden by Aliah and His Apostle, nor acknwoledge the religion of Truth (even if they are) of the people of the Book, until they pay the Jizyah with willing submission and feel themselves subdued.

-Al Quran IX : 29

Here in this verse feel subdued means that they should surrender arms and acknowledge the supremacy of the Islamic state.

Sunnah also includes that the Prophet realized Jizyah from the Maqil fo Baharin. Similarly, the rightly guided caliphs realized Jizyah from people of the Book and others like them in all the conquered territories. And this practice continued until it came to be ijma or consensus of the ummah.

Khiraj is that revenue, which after the conquest of a country was levied on its arable lands. These lands had been left in posession of the original owners; and according to this productivity at a fixed rate (for example

128

one fourth) according to an agreed weight or measure cereals or price, thereof was realized as khiraj. Coming to consider this khiraj, it must be kept in view that since the Muslim owners of land have to pay zakat on the produce of their fields (Ushr - one tenth or one twentieth of the total produce on non-irrigated or rain-fed and irrigated lands), which non-Muslims do not have to pay and have to pay khiraj in lieu of it. If the owner of such (khiraj paying) lands embraced Islam, or a Muslim purchased this land from a zimmi, he had to pay khiraj all the same. Imam Abu Haneefah, his disciples (Imam Abu Yusuf and Imam Muhammad), Imam Laith bin Sad Imam Sha'bi and Ikramullah are reported to have expressed their opinions. According to other Imams in such a situation the Muslim owner of land will have to pay zakat (Ushr) also on his agricultural produce.

-See *Al Amwal* p. 91 and *Al Musannif* Vol. III p. 201

Those who pay superficial attention to these things, easily fall a prey to the misunderstanding, particularly in case of Jizyah. However, looking about more searchingly, it will become evident that Islam has not been any the less considerate in the matter of justice.

Islam has made compulsory military service binding on the Muslims. And the defence of the country is closely associated with it even if they are residents of the neighbouring areas of the Islamic state. The non-Muslims have been exempted from it, even if they are living under the protection of the Islamic state (involved in Jehad).

The basic cause lies in the fact that the Islamic state is ideological based on principles and ideology. Its protection can be undertaken by those only who believe in this principle and ideology. How much sensible and how far justifiable can it be that one, who regards them totally false, be compelled to lay down his life for its protection? Again, how his own religion will permit him to fight from an alien religion that he regards antagonistic to his own?

That is why Islam has totally restricted the obligation of Jihad to the Muslims, since it is a sacred religious duty and a devotional act through which a Muslim can get closer to his Lord and cherisher, Allah, so much so that the reward reserved for a mujahid is much greater than that of the abstinent and devout persons constantly engaged in prayer and other devotional acts.

To make other non-Muslims participate in the defence of the country, and meeting in some degree the cost of defence,. they have been compelled to pay a tax technically known as jizyah. So, the reality and nature of jizyah if only this much that it is the monetary recompense for military service and not a sign of submission to the Muslim authority and rule in humility.

It is for this reason that it has been levied on only those combat fit men, women, children and those incapable of earning being totally exempted. The utterance of Umar Farooq is well known : "Do not levy jizyah on women and children." The jurists are of the opinion that if a woman works to enter Darul Islam on payment of jizyah she should be permitted to enter, and settle, but the amount of her jizyah should be returned to her, since it is not permitted. However, if she offers that amount as a contribution to her new country, knowing full well that jizyah is not realized from women, it may be accepted. Old and decrepit persons, blind and cripples are also bracketted with women and children since they are unable to take up arms like them.

As a demonstration of tolerance, the friars in the monasteries have also been granted exemption since they too do not takeup arms.

-See *Matalib Ulin Nuha*, VIII, P. 96

The western historian Adam Metz writes :

The zimmis taking advantage of the tolerance of Muslims and the protection proved by them, paid jizyah, everyone according to his capacity. This jizyah resembeld the tax for national defense and only the combatfit paid it. Cripples, in capacitated, the ascelis and devotees in the monsteries were totally exempt from it.

-*Islami Tehzeeb*, Vol.I P. 96.

Another reason for levy of jizyah on zimmis -and this is the argument which every government in every age has sought support in, namely the expenses on public welfare, for example, policing, judiciary with courts, and public works like construction, of roads, bridges, so essential for improvement of economy, and from which every citizen, Muslim and non-Muslim derives benefit. The Muslim take part in this kind of expenditure through payment of zakat and other sadaqat like sadaqah fitr and other taxes. The participation in this behalf on the part of non-Muslims with their petty tax - Jizyah - should be no wonder. That is why in Maliki Fiqah the ordainments relating to Jizyah have been taken up with those of zakat.

-See *Risalah Ibn Abi Zaid* with explanatory notes, Vol. I. P. 331

WHEN JIZYAH BECOMES UNJUSTIFIABLE

As we have stated earlier jizyah is the tax paid in return of the protection of life and property provided by the Islamic state to its zimmi subjects. If the Islamic set up fails to provide this protection, it forfeits its right to realization of jizyah from them.

This was the situtation that practically confronted the Muslim armies in Syria at several places. They received news from his own independent source that hostile armies of Roman's (christians) were gathering to attack them in Syria. They thought of leaving that various places of Sojewn and concentrate at a strategic place. But before that those who have paid jizyah they told their lower staff, must get it back since they would not be able to provide protection to them for some time. And they should be told very clearly, no protection no jizyah. After some time, Allah willing, they may come back and restore other conditions of the pact and offering protection once again, jizyah will become acceptable.

Khalid and many other commanders had given the zimmis in many pacts in writing that if they were able to provide them protection they would be entitled to receive jizyah from them, otherwise not. *-Tarikh-e-Tabri*

Similarly, if the zimmis participates in the war against the enemies of Islam shoulder to shoulder with the Muslims of Darul Islam, they will be exempted from payment of jizyah. During the period of Umar, the pacts that were signed between the Muslims and the zimmis, several of them in clear terms mentioned this discontinuation of jizyah for participation in the protection of Darul Islam - which was their own country as well.

-See*Ahkamuz-zimmieen wal Mustamineen*,
Dr. Abdul Karim Zaidan, P. 155

In the agreement signed between the representatives of Abu Ubaidah with the Jarajimah Christians, it was agreed that this would help the Muslims and keep them informed of the movements of the enemies.

-*Futuhul Buldan-Al Balazari*, P. 217

The method of collecting jizyah was that once in a year it was realized in the form of cash or kind or even goods. However, wine, dead animal, or pigs were not accepted. Umar had issued instructions to give rope to the zimmis in this behalf, "One who is incapable of paying jizyah, leave him alone. One who is constrained or in great distress, help him, since it is not a matter of only a year or two. So it is noticed realization of jizyah was at times delayed so that in the harvesting season it may become easy to pay.

-*Akhamus-Sultaniah*, Mawardi, P. 138,
Tarikh-e-Damishq, Ibn Asakir, Vol. I, P.
178, Al Amwel, P. 44

The Islamic state adopted a policy of gentleman and kind-heartedness in the realization of jizyah. Once when an officer of his on duty presented his collection of jizyah before Umar Farooq, he felt that it was in exces of what was due from them. He remarked rather reproachingly. "It appears you have ruined those people (you could lay hands on)". That officer replied, "By Allah : we have realized it with utmost gentleness". Umar further aksed, "Without strictness, compulsion and use of force? The officer replied in the affirmative. At this, Umar expressing his satisfaction remarked, "Thanks are due to Allah that he neither let me commit any oppression or excess, nor anyone else in my sphere of authority.

Umar had levied a commercial tax on the zimmis which was realized once a year, at 5% of the total cost of goods, for taking it from one country to another. In the modern termionlogy it can be called custom duty. From Muslim traders it was calculated at 2½% for the purpose of their payment of zakat, and from the traders of Darul Harbit was 10%, since the Muslims had also to pay at the same rate in their countries. Ziyed bin Husair on being asked had replied that since the residents of dar-ul-harb charged them at the same rate so they paid them in the same coin.

-At-merat, P. 706

Realization of 5% trade tax was also in corporated in the conditions of the contracts signed during the period of Umar with zimmis. Some ulama of the Hanafite school of Fiqh are of the opinion that this tax was levied for their protection. And since there were greater chances of misadventures at the hands of robbers and thieves where zimmis' goods was concerned, that protection involved too fold of that alertness and action needed for Muslim trade so trade tax which in reality was protection tax was for this reason of their greater value-ability charged at a higher rate.

-Sharah-ul-Ghayah Alal Hidayah, Vol. I. P. 532

Maulana Maudoodi has opinion that the Muslims were mostly engaged in the defence of the Islamic state, trade was totally in the hands of the zimmis. So the jurists for the sake of Muslim traders' interest and by way of encouragement to them in this field, reduced their trade tax.

-The rights of zimmis in an Islamic state, P. 25

Anyway, the jurists had taken this decision on the basis of Umar's action in this behalf. In this connection no Quranic verse or tradition of the Prophet is available, and so Umar in view of the expediencies of the state had taken this step and its inclusion in the treaties of peace also was for this reason.

Dr. Abdul Karim Zaidan has written that the trade tax on Muslims, compared to the zimmis was reduced for the reason that barring this trade tax levied on goods, taken from the one country to another, neither there was any tax on a zimmi's commercial goods, nor any on the wealth accummulated by him in the form of silver and gold, nor yet the produce of his fields and cattle were taxable, whereas Muslims had to pay zakat on all those things and in this way they were over-burdened financially. But since zakat is a devotional act involving ones goods the zimmis were exempt from it.[16]

---

16. Maulana Syed Muhammad Miyan (of late lamented memory) has writen in his book, "*Ulama-e-Hind ka Shandar Mazi.*" Vol I., P. 562-575.

Here this distinction is clearly visible that from a Muslim only half that (of zimmi) one fortieth or 2½% is realized.

In this way there appears to be some allowance (reduction in the rate of tax) in the case of a Muslim. But along with that if the other aspect is kept in view this remission will appear illusory.

The fact is that this one twentieth is realized from the non-Muslims for their commercial goods. Besides that he may have thousands, even millions in cash or in the form of gold, and silver jewellery and other articles, nothing is charged for it.

On the contrary a Muslim's wealth whether it is with him or has been lent out to others, zakat has a claim on it.

For example, take a Muslim and a non-Muslim with a capital of hundred thousand in this way that twenty thousand is invested in trade, fifty thousand is hard cash with the owner, and thirty thousand with others as debts. In such a situation from the non-Muslim one twentieth of twenty thousand or one thousand can be taken as tax. But from the Muslim one fortieth of his entire assets including the thirty thousand lent out, shall be taken away from him, which comes to two thousand five hundred. And over and above the zakat there are other dues of an obligatory nature and on a Muslim which are also to be taken into account.

1.   Expenditure of war is the responsibility of·the Muslims to be met from their own resources. For, where they are in authority and rule, the protection of the country and the citizens is the obligatory duty of the Muslims. And for this purpose whatever endeavours, initiatory or one of advancement or purely defensive in nature, it is known in the terminology of the Shariah, as Jihad. And Jihad is an obligatory devotional act for Muslims. And just all the responsibilities of jihad too come to their shoulders. The expenditure of war cannot be transferred to the non-Muslims as a matter of principle but only as a matter of cooperation and mutual help. If they refuse to cooperate in this behalf they are not rebels or unfaithful to the Islamic side.

2.   If the Muslims are the owners of cattle, cows, oxen, goats, sheep, camels and horses, zakat will be due and realized from➲

It can be asserted that the amount of money realized from zimmis as jizyah and khiraj becomes equal to that realized from Muslims under various heads. But the Khiraj on land is not specific to zimmis. If a zimmi embraces Islam or a Muslim purchases a zimmi's land. Khiraj shall continue as of old, change of creed of the owner of land or change c ͭ hands in its possession making no difference whatsoever. However, jizyah is specific to zimmis. But it is a nominal tax and is not taxing to them at all. And even that petty sum is not obligatory for every one. Only the combat-fit able bodied young men are made to pay it. And in case of taking up military service they too are exempted.

-Ahkamul Zimmieen wal Muntamineen, P. 186

Again, if the situation changes and a zimmi too has to pay taxes on all his assets (cattle, produce of the field, cash, gold, silver and commercial goods) equal in

---

⊃them. The details are to be found in the books on Fiqh. But the non-Muslims are exempted from it. It is a devotional act for Muslims not just a tax on property of every citizen.

3.　Every Muslim if he has the means, must pay Sadaqah Fitr at the close of Ramadhan and sacrifies some animal on 10th Zul Hijjah every year.

4.　In particular situations like intentionally breaking a fast in Ramadhan or violation of an oath, to make amends a Muslim has to pay a penalty involving expenditure of money. This also takes the form of an obligatory duty involving money.

5.　A Muslim cannot undertake business of selling wine and swine. For the purchase and sale of gold and silver, certain curbs have been placed on him. The non-Muslims are perfectly free to take to any of these trades.

6.　Muslims who can afford to travel to Makkah after provision has been made for their dependents during the period of their absence, Hajj is an obligatory duty (a devotion act) for them once in a life time, which takes a considerable amount of money.

amount to that paid by a Muslim as zakat, a zimmi trader and a Muslim businessman may be charged with an equal amount of the tax.

GENERAL LAWS

Since zimmis are the citizens of the Islamic state, those laws that have nothing to do with the religion or their freedom shall be binding on them as well. The devotional acts of Muslims or those that have a religious significance such as zakat which is a military service as also an Islamic obligatory function, can not be enforced on them. For this reason Jizyah was imposed on them in lieu of zakat so that their religious feelings may not be injured. Zimmis are perfectly free to follow the dictates of their religion in matters relating to their families and social affairs even if these matters be prohibited in Islam, such as the laws and ceremonies relating to marriage, and divorce and those involving wine and pigs. Islam never put any restrictions on them. They are free to act on whatever they regard permitted.

Islam neither prevents a fire worshiper from marrying woman eternally prohibited, nor a Jew marrying his neice, nor does it deprive Christians from drinking and eating pork. If they regard these permitted Islam does not meddle in these affairs.

However, if the zimmis bring their case to the Islamic court, the jurists are of the opinion that a decision can be given according to the Islamic Shariah. The Quran says :

If they do come to thee, either judge between them

or decline to interfere. If thou decline they can not hurt thee in the least. If thou judge, judge then inequity between them. For Allah loveth those who judge in equity.

-Al Quran V. : 45

That is why there are separate courts for the zimmis. The western historian, Adam Metz writes :

Since the Islamic Shariah specifically governed the affairs of the Muslims, the followers of other religions were free to institute special courts for themselves. This type of Christian courts functioned under the Christian learned men. In this connection they had many books on law compiled by these erudites. They dealt mostly with marriage, inheritance and those other matters that could crop among themselves. The Islamic state had nothing to do with those affairs. The Christians has also the right to seek justice at the Islamic courts. But the clergy did not approve of it. In Egypt the Qazis had a day fixed for the Christians and on that particular day only their cases were taken up. In 177 A.H. when Qazi Muhammed bin Masrooq was appointed Qazi of Egypt, he started hearing of their cases in the mosque itself. Where Spain is concerned, it is learnt from reliable sources that Christians decided their own cases, taking only cases of murder to the Qazis

-Islami Thaqafat Chauthi Sadi Hijri men

Affairs other than these which in degree related to religion, for example, murder, that etc. theft rules applying to the Muslims were also applied to zimmis; if zimmi committed theft or was found guilty of highway robbery or had committed muder or devoured somebody's goods or fornicated or slandered some innocent woman, in such crimes Islamic limits were enforced on the culprits.

Imam Abu Haneefah is of the opinion that the zimmis, male or female can be punished for fornication or adultery only by flogging. They cannot be stoned to death, since *rajm* (stoning to death) is associated with Islam.

The same principle will apply to financial matters, for example sale and purchase hiring and lathering on hire, mortgages, agriculture and trade agreements and possession, use, disposal etc. The sale and purchase of things permissible to Muslims in a particular manner, is also permissible to the zimmis and the way it will be prohibited for Muslims it will be likewise unpermissible for them too. However wine and swine have been kept out of it because they are permitted by the Christian religion. Only it will have to be carefully observed that their deals should not be open.

Since the interest is prohibited in their religion too, it was not exempted in their case. It is expected of the non-Muslims too that living in a Muslim society, they would have regard for their feelings. For example, they will not be allowed to revile Islam, the Prophet of Islam and the Quran publicly or propagate such beliefs and ideologies which are not part of their religion. For example, Trinity and Cross etc. with reference to the Christian religion. Similarly they should have regard for it that those things that are prohinited in Islam such as wine and pork should not be used publicly. They are not permitted to sell these things to Muslims since this will create complications in the Muslim society.

Similarly they should exercise care in the matter of taking food and drinks in the month of Ramadhan openly, since it will be a disagreeable sight for the fasting Muslim community.

Whatever Islam disapproves but is permitted by Christianity they will have to keep in view only this much that they should abstain from public demonstration of the same, so that there may be no unpleasantness created in the society and all of them should be able to live together in peace and amity.

Urfah bin Harith who had participated with Ikramah bin Abu Jehal in fighting against apostasy in Yemen, reports that he called a Christian to the Islamic faith, and he as a reaction reproached the Apostle of Allah. When this matter came before Umro bin As, he said that since they had entered a pact with them, nothing could be done against them in that situation. Urfah said, "I seek refuge in Allah : We did not enter agreements with them that they should revile Allah and his Apostle. We are bound only in as much as we do not stand between them and their places of worship, do not cast heavy burden on them that they can not bear and fight for their protection and leave them unhindered to decide matters according to their own religious dictators. Umro bin As said, "You have uttered the very truth".

-See Tabrani

CHAPTER III

UNIQUE TOLERANCE

Serveral types of religious and ideological tolerance have been witnessed. One type is that in which you give freedom to the followers of other religions in matters of creed and faith. You do not compell them to accept your religion by force nor punish them in various ways in this connection, but do provide them facilities and amenities that they may meet their religious duties with perfect satisfaction and freedom, and keep away from those things which their religion disallow.

Another type of tolerance is that you allow the followers of other religions perfect rights and freedoms to subscribe to any creed he likes, and strictly observe the permitted and prohibited of his religion, and in this connection he may not feel any sort of constraint due to your behaviour. For example the Jews cannot force them to work on these days of the week against the dictates of their religion. If a Christian goes to church on Sundays, he cannot be made to work on Sundays against the practice of his own religion.

But these things are related to matters that are not in direct conflict with your own religion. The greatest tolerance is this that you do not let the followers of other religions feel constrained in those things that in your own religion are strictly prohibited but permitted in theirs.

The Muslims had all along practised this last magnificent, degrees of tolerance in thier relations with zimmis.

Whatever the non-Muslim regarded permitted by his religion the Islamic state gave perfect latitude for that and never constrained it by imposing restrictions on it, when it would have been in its rights to do so according to the faith and the laws of the state, particularly in a situation when something has been permitted by a certain religion but not declared obligatory for its own followers. For example if in the religion of a Cuebra marrying a real sister might have been permitted but it is not binding on any one. He can marry another woman in spite of permission to marry his real sister. Or for example, a christian is permitted by his religion to eat pork but it does not make it obligatory and he can easily have on other animals' flesh also. Or if the Bible permits drinking, the Christian community is not under any obligation to drink.

But Islam did nothing of the sort. Whatever the non-Muslims regarded permitted, Islam did not try to create any constraint on it but said to the Muslims that they should give them perfect freedom to act according to their religion.

Then there are things that neither come under any law nor can any government enforce them. In such things human feelings, polite manners in social gatherings, allowance to a neighbour, broad mindedness and generosity in dealings, piety and doing a good turn and kind-heartedness alone can demonstrate the spirit of tolerance. Such things we come upon in life and no law or a judicial court can influence them. This spirit and passion for tolerance has perhaps never been witnessed in any non-Muslims society. This demonstration of finer feelings and sensitivity of the Islamic tolerance has been oft-repeated and witnessed during the blessed periods of their authority and rule in the history of the world.

About such polytheist parents who have been constantly trying to take away their Muslim son back to polytheism the Quran instructs the son:

> Yet bear their company in their life with justice (and consideration).
>
> -Al Quran XXXI : 15.

For the opponent who do not take up arms against the Muslims the Quran commands the Muslims to have dealings based on justice and piety with them:

> Allah forbids you not with regard to those who fight you not for (your) faith, nor drive you out of your houses, from dealing kindly and justly with them for Allah Loveth those who are just.
>
> -Al Quran IX : 8

Landing the righteous and kind-hearted Muslims the Quran says :

> And they feed for the love of Allah, the indigent, the orphan and the captive.
>
> -(Q. XXXVI : 8)

When this verse was revealed, the captives were from among the polytheists.

The Quran in trying to remove the Muslim's doubts about spending on their pagan relatives and neighbours, instructs them thus :

> It is not required of thee (O Apostle), to set them on the right path but Allah sets on the right path when He pleaseth. Whatever of goods you give, benefits your own souls, and you shall only do so seeking the "Face of Allah."   -Al Quran II : 272

Imam Muhammad bin Hasan reports that when famine overtook Makkah, the Apostle of Allah had sent goods and commodities to be distributed among the indigent of that town when Makkah had done to him and to his companions what it had done.

-Sharah-us-Seer-ul Kabeer, Vol. I, p. 144.

Asma bint Abi Bakr reports that her pagan mother visited her. She asked the Apostle of Allah whether she could do any thing for her by way of kind-heartedness to blood-relations. The Prophet instructed her to do it (and generously too).

-Tafseer Ibn Katheer, Vol. IV, p.349.

The manners and etiquettes of engaging in discussion with the adversaries, the Quran taught thus :

And dispute ye not with the people of the Book except with means better (than mere disputation), unless it be with those of them who inflict wrong (and injury) but says, "We believe in the revelation which has come down to us and in that which came down to you: our Allah and your Allah is one: -Quran XXIX : 46.

We notice the glimpse of tolerance in the relations of good neighbourly treatment and behaviour of the Prophet with the Jews and the Christians (who were the only non-Muslims there with him). He used to go to them, did good neighbourly treatment to them and dealt with them civilly, visiting the sick among them, and had dealings of give and take also with them.

Ibn Ishaq has quoted a report that the delegation from Najran came to the Prophet at Madinah. It was an exclusively Christian delegation. They entered the Prophet's mosque about the time of late afternoon (asr) prayer. And when the time of their prayer approached they stood up there for prayer. People wanted to stop them from so doing, but the Prophet did not approve of this (restriction), saying, "Leave them alone." So they offered their prayers facing. Al Bait-ul-Muqdis. Ibn Qayyim commenting on this incident has written that it proves that the People of the Book can enter a Muslim mosque and offer their prayers too in the presence of the Muslims. However, it is a casual incident and can not be made the basis of a regular practice and a general law (casually it may be allowed again).

-Zad-ul Ma'ad, Vol. III

Abu Ubaid has reported from Saeed bin-ul Musayyib that the Apostle of Allah had given something to a Jewish family as sadaqah (an act of charity). So the practice (of giving sadaqah to the People of the Book) continues to this day.   *-Al-Amwal,* p. 63.

Anas has reported in Bukhari that the Apostle of

Allah visited a Jew in his sick-bead and called him to Islam, which he embraced. He came out saying, "Allah must be thanked that He saved him from hell-fire making me the means of it."

Bukhari has also reported that a coat of mail of the Prophet about the time of his death was mortgaged with a Jew. This loan he had taken for the expenses of the family. He could have very easily borrowed this paltry sum from his companions but in this way he was leaving a healthy tradition for the ummah.

The Apostle of Allah used to accept gifts from non-Muslims,and both in war and peace he has taken help from them (Non-Muslims).

A funeral procession passed by the Prophet and he stood up as a mark of respect for it. He was told that the bier was that of a Jew. He replied, "Was he not a human being."

The same type of excellent toleration is reflected in the lives of the companions also.

Umar, the second rightly guided caliph, sanctioned regular aid (as charity) for a Jewish family from the Bait-ul-mal and pronouncing (for the instruction of the millat): "Allah says : Alms are for the poor and the needy. (Q.IX : 60) and he is one of these needy from the People of the Book."

-Al Khiraj, p.26.

Umar passes by some paupers on his journey to Syria and he orders help for them from the Bait-ul-Mal.

When Umar was fatally wounded by a Cuebre zimmi, Abu Lu Loo, from his death bed he gives instructions to his probable successors (election not yet over) to treat zimmis kindly, to abide by the laws of agreements with them, fighting for their protection and not to cast greater burden on them than they could bear.

Bukhari, Baihaqi

Ibn Umar repeatedly instructs his servant to take the meat of a sacrificial animal to the neighbouring Jewish family. The servant asks him the reason for this unusual attention paid to a Jew and receives the following answer. "The Apostle of Allah said, that Gabriel (Allah's messenger to the prophets) so often kept inviting his attention to the care of the neighbours that he came to think of the neighbour being made partner in inheritance."

A Christian woman Umme Harith bin Rabiah dies. The companions of the Prophet join the funeral procession.

-Fiqh-uz-Zakat

Some of the very astonishing persons among the followers of the companions used to give from Sadaqah fitr to the Christian zimmis and felt there was nothing wrong with it. Rather some very important men from them like Ikramah bin Seereen and Zahri found no fault in paying them from zakat. When Jabir bin Zaid was asked "Whom to give zakat?" he had replied, "To the Muslims and their zimmis

-Al Muhalli, Ibn Hazam, Vol. V, p 117.

Qazi Aiyaz has written in Tarteeb-ul-Madarik, that Dar Qutumi has reported an incident that once a vizier of the Abbasid caliph, Muhazid Billah, Abdoon bin Said, a Christian came to Qazi Ismail bin Ishaq (An outstanding jurist of the Malikite school of Fiqh). The Qazi received him and stood up to pay respect to him. Noting the signs of disapproval on the faces of the gathering around him he said after the departure of the said vizier, Allah says:

Allah only forbids you, with regard to those who fought you for (your) Faith, drive you out of your houses, and support others in driving you out, from burning them for friendship and protection). It is such as turn to them (in these circumstances) that do wrong. (Q.LX : 8)

And this person meets the needs of the Muslims and serves as an intermediary between ourselves and the caliph. So whatever I did according to this Quranic verse falls under acts of charity and goodness.

The Imams (religious leaders) and jurists in defence of zimmis and the protection of their honour and dignity, like that of Muslims have been coming years and again as you might seen in the incidents relating to Imam Auza'i and Imam ibn Taimiyah.

The well known jurist and researcher, Allamah Shahabuddin Qarani, in explaining the word 'Bir' (goodness) writes that Allah has ordered doing good to the non Muslims. It includes gentlemen to their weaker elements, meeting the needs of those who are unable to do it themselves, feeding the hungry and clothing the naked, speaking gently and politely to them, out of kindness and civility and not due to fear and humility. If they are neighbours disagreeable things from them must be put up with even if one has the poser to stop them from doing it. One should also pray for their guidance to the right path and that they may come to belong to the group of the blessed ones. We must wish well by them in every thing relating to them, temporal and spiritual. Similarly their secrets should be guarded, their distress removed from them, their lives, properties and honour and dignity and rights and interests must be protected. They must be saved from oppression and their (usurped) rights restored to them. All these are covered by the divine commandment of doing good.

-Al-Furuq, Vol. III, p.15

The basis of Muslims' tolerant treatment of the non-Muslims are those realities and ideologies that Islam has firmly set in the minds of the Muslims. The most important among them are these :

1. Every Muslim believes in the honour and prestige of man, no matter what his religion, sex and colour.

Allah says :

We have honoured the sons of Adam. (Q. XVII : 70)

This honour conferred by Allah on man makes it obligatory for us to respect him and give him some allowances. That is why when a funeral procession passed by the Apostle of Allah he stood up out of respect for man. And when he was informed that was a dead body of a Jew, he quietened them by saying, "Was he not a man? He thereby imparted the education that every human life is worth of respect. How lofty the truth and how beautiful the saying:

2. A Muslim has a firm belief that creed is a matter of divine dispensation and differences of religious creeds are just as Allah willed, giving man at the same time the freedom of choice in the following words:

Let him who will believe, and let him who will reject (if).   -Al Quran XVIII : 29

And, If thy Lord had so willed, he could have made mankind one people: but they will not cease to dispute.   -Al Quran XI : 118

And it is apparent, no one can change the will of Allah. And Allah wills only that which is full of goodness and wisdom, man may or may not come to know it. So a Muslim can never even imagine that he should convert all the Non-Muslims to Islam by force, when Allah has reminded His Apostle of this well-known truth:

If it had been thy Lords will, they would have all believed, all who are on earth:

-Al Quran X : 99

3. Muslims have not been compelled to call the unbelievers to account for their unbelief or chase misguided for their misguidance. This is neither their responsibility nor this world is the appropriate place for any stock-taking. Allah alone shall call them to account for their deeds. And for that accountability Dooms day has been fixed long since :

If they do wrangle with thee, say, "Allah knows best what it is ye are doing." Allah will judge between you on the Day of Judgement concerning the matters in which ye differ.

-Al Quran XXII : 68-69

Addressing His Apostle Allah says about the people of the Book.

Now then, for that (reason), call (them to the faith), and stand steadfast, as thou curt commanded, nor follow thou their aim desires, but say, I believe in the Book which Allah has sent down, and I am commanded to judge just between you. Allah is our Lord and your Lord: For us (is the responsibility for) our deeds, and for you for your deeds. There is no contention between us and you, Allah will bring us together, and to Him is (our) final return.

-Al Quran XLII : 15

In the light of these circumstances man's conscience is perfectly at ease, and he is not at all torn between the non-Muslims' false creed and leaving him along with his creed, affairs and all, and doing good to him- no religions struggle between these two contradictory elements disturbs his peace of mind.

4.   The Muslim believes firmly that Allah enjoins justice and equity and approves of it too. Similarly, He commands him to lofty morals, even if it is in dealing

with former polytheists. He disapproves of oppression and tyranny, and punishes the oppressors and tyrants even if perpetrated by Muslims on unbelievers.

And let not the hatred of others to you make you swerve to wong and depart from justice. Be just, that is next to piety:

And the Apostle of Allah himself has said:

Between the piteous cry of the oppressed - to whichever religion he may belong - and Allah there is no obstruction.

-*Musnad Imam Ahmad*

CHAPTER IV
SOME MISUNDERSTANDINGS

In spite of the shining examples of justice and equity, and tolerance in the Islamic history, we find that the opponents tried to tarnish the fair face of Islam in many ways and created all sorts of mis-givings and doubts about it. The orientalists in particular, tried to black paint the bright face of Islamic history, whereas if they had done justice to Islam and the Islamic peoples in the light of its historical background and historical facts, no misunderstandings could have been created.

Jizyah was the greatest target in this vehement campaign of maligning Islam, presenting it in such an ugly and dreadful form that the word itself came to be a menacing term to the non-Muslims, conveying to them the idea of disgrace and ignominy. Whereas Jizyah, as we have already made it clear, had been imposed on non-Muslims, living under the protection of an Islamic state, in lieu of zakat and Jehad, the two most important devotional acts as well as duty and tax on Muslims. And these were not imposed on non-Muslims since they were religious in their nature. However, if the zimmis partake with the Muslims in military service and defence of the country they became exempted from Jizyah. Similarly, tax equivalent to zakat can be realized from zimmis so that their participation in providing finances for the country they may be putting up on the basis of equality, no matter whether it is called zakat (or by some other name in their case), to avoid creation of sensitivity in them with regard to the religious aspect of zakat. If the non-Muslims wince or allergy to this word Jizyah it can be given some other name, for it is not this word that is important but the purpose it serves Umar Ibn Khattab himself realized Jizyah from Bani Tughlab in the name of zakat.

Here we are going to present the quotation from the book of a famous English author, Sir Thomas Arnold, '*Preaching of Islam*', which will go a long way in removing the misunderstanding.

"The purpose of imposing this tax, jizyah on Christians - as some of them misunderstood - was not the punishment of their abstaining from entering the fold of Islam but they (the Christians) paid this tax with other zimmis, in return for the protection offer to them by the Muslim swords, since the military service (defence) they could not undertake on grounds of religion. So when the citizens of Heerah paid their amount of Jizyah, they clearly declared that they were paying it on condition that Muslims and their Amir will protect them from Muslims and other people."

The pact entered into by Khalid bin Waleed with the people in the neighbourhood of Heerah clearly mentioned that if they were in a position to help them, shall be entitled to realize Jizyah from them, otherwise not. This very vivid condition is proved also by the incident when during the Caliphate of Umar, the Roman emperor started gathering a vast army against the Muslims on the Syrian front, the Muslims too had to concentrate their forces. The Muslim supreme commander issued instructions to the conquered portion of Syriya to return the amount of Jizyah realised from them and have it declared that the situation is such that they could not protect them from external aggression or internal harm, and so were returning to them the amounts realized from them. "If by the grace of Allah we return victorious to you, we shall accept once again the resposibilities of the contract". So a very large amount of money was returned to the zimmis. And the Christians prayed for the Muslims that they should return victorious to them, "If the Romans (Christians) had been in your place", they said, "They would have never returned anything to us. Rather, they would have snatched everything from us, they could lay hands on".

- Kitabul Khiraj, Ibn Yusuf, P. 81.

As already mentioned Jizyah was imposed on combat-fit young males. And in return for it military service, obligatory for Muslims along with payment of Zakat, was written off. However, if they opted for participation in defence of the country with the Muslims it would exempt them from Jizyah. They would be entitled to spirit of war and other amenities like Muslim mujahids.

- Bilazari, P. 159.

In 22 A.H. when the Islamic conquerors bordered on Iran, there too an agreement on similar terms was signed by the commander of the Muslim armies.

- Tabrani, Vol. I, P. 2665

The non-Muslims employed in the Uthmani Turkish armies were exempted from Jizyah. The Christians of Maghris in Albania were exempted from Jizyah on condition that they would provide armed men for the frontier of (mountain) passes between Cithaeron and Ceraned hills. The non-Muslims serving in the Turkish army or in construction work, were not only exempt from payment of khiraj but rent free lands were also allotted to them.

- *Marsegli*, Vol. I, P. 86

The citizens of Hydre too did not pay any tax to Sultan. Rather, they had provided two hundred and fifty persons for the Royal Navy, who were paid from Baitul Mal for their support.

- *Fenley*, Vol. VI : P. 30-32

The Ermetols of South Rumania who were an important element of Turkish armier, in the sixteenth and seventeenth centuries and the Christian tribe of Merdite was exempted from Jizyah on condition that in a state of war they would furnish armed fighting men to the Turkish army to form a double division.

- *De Le Janquire*, P. 14

Similarly jizyah had been remitted in the case of Christians from Greece who protected water supplied to constantinople or kept watch over the gun-powder stocks of the town, since they were engaged in military service.

- *Thomas Smith*, P. 324 and *Dros Thomas*, P. 326

As contrasted with them, the Egyptian cultivators

(Fallahin) who were Muslims had been exempted form military service and like Christians had to pay jizyah.

- De La Jonquire, P. 265

There is also another wide-spread misunderstanding about putting a seal on or branding zimmis. And it has been presented in such a way that it was a permanent mark on a zimmi and this system had been a Muslim invention to disgace them, whereas this allegation has been falsified by the orientalists.

Tertone writes in his book "zimmi in Islam".

According to the historian Yaqoobi, a seal was put on them only at the time of realization of jizyah (to eliminate mistakes in payment), and once it was over, the seal was removed. Qazi Abu Yusuf writes that seal should be put at the time of realization of Jizyah and once the counting with identification is over it should be done away with. Again, to be just and equitous, it is not an invention of the Arabs. They had only taken it up from others and practiced it.

Dr. Kharbotali has written that the Muslims had borrowed the system of putting seals on zimmis at the time of realization of Jizyah from the Romans (Christians) and its purpose was not debasing them (the zimmis) but that those who had paid their dues should be easily identified, and there may be no irregularities, errors and contentions. Printing in that period had not made such advances as could make it possible to introduce. The system of issuing receipt. Therefore keeping a correct account presented difficulties. Even in the twentieth century in many Asian and African countries an uncouth system of marking the fingers of a voter with an indelible ink to eliminate illegal practices (like voting of one person more than once for absentees). The stain of this ink wears off in a few days.

-Islam and Ahle zimmah, P. 84-85

A misunderstanding also exists about the dress and their (zimmis) mode of living and moving about. It is said about Umar, the second rightly guided caliph, that he had imposed restrictions on zimmis that they should not seek resemblances to the Muslims in their dress and manners. Their dress must have something distinctive which could mark them out quite apart from the Muslims. The same has been allegedly reported about the Umayyid, Caliph Umar bin Abdul Aziz.

Many orientalists have declared such a report about Umar doubtful, since the early reliable historians of that period like Tabari, Blazari, Ibn Atheer and Yaqoobi do not mention it in their books. However, instead of refuting it outright, what is needed is to find out the reasons behind it.

Such instructions do not have any religious significance and hence no permanence. Rather, they had been given in a particular period in keeping with the expediency and need of a particular society. With the change of conditions and the situation it did automatically become obsolete and unnecessary.

The truth about it is that in that age some distinction between people according to their religions were necessary, since the followers of every religion themselves demanded it Dress and modes of carrying themeselves were the only means of distinction that could be easily adopted for this purpose. In that early period there were no identity cards. Therefore to distinguish the followers of one religion from another, these instructions were issued. That is why in the present age, no jurist regards it necessary since there is no need of it.

Dr. Kharbotaly writes :

Even if, for the sake of discussion we take it as reliable that the two caliphs had issued instructions like these, there was nothing wrong with it, for in that early period of history when there were no such things as identity cards giving any trace of citiszenship, religion, age, etc., dress was the only outstanding distinguishing feature which could make out separately the followers of any particular religion. The Arabs and the Muslims too had instructions to this effect (to adopt the dress and the mode of living and moving about whic could distinguish them from others). Similar instructions were issued to the Christians, Jews and Guebres, (Magii). If the orientalists say that it was injustice and a hardship to them, it was similar for both of them, since (not one but) all of them had instructions to avoid resemblance to one another.

- Islam and Ahle Zimmah, P. 816-87

The historian Tertone expessing his opinion about it writes that the regulations relating to the dress were introduced to make distinction between the Arabs and the Christians easy. And there is no room for any doubt in this behalf. Abu Yusuf and Ibn Abdul Hakam have definitely mentioned it.

- Kitabul Khiraj, P. 72 Futuhul Misr, P. 151

And the Christians had taken to it of their own accord. Later, such a distinction came also to be considered necessary when the Arabs had developed a cultuer of their own and the subject nations had started imitating them in this field too.

Any way this regulation and restriction about dress, general appearance and carriage lasted for a limited brief span and most often its enforcement was neglected and compiance overlooked. Nor was there any complaint or protect against it in that period. History bears testimony to this fact.

The Christian poet Akhtal (D. 95 A.H.) entered the royal presence of the Ummayid caliph Abdul Malik Bin Merwan clad in silk, a cross dangling from his nech and drops of liquoridripping from his lips, and wetting his long beard. And the caliph used to receive him warmly. The christians of Jarajiniah tribe of thehilly tracts of Syrai used to dress in the style of Muslims.

- Futuh-ul- Buldan, P. 161

Qazi Abu Yusuf has emphasized a distinguishing dress form the non-Muslims. And that too for identification in which compulsion and use of force were out of question.

Those subscribing to other religions lived in perfect

161

peace amity, honour and freedom in a Muslim society, which has been acknowledged even by the justice-loving writers of the west. However, some authors picking up rare incidents, not many in number, have tied to spread misunderstandings also when it is known that such incidents were doings of common ignorant people under certain particular conditions and such mistakes are common in every society even today. The reason for these incidents was that Islamic tolerance had provided the zimmis opportunities to thoroughly pervade the financial and administrative departments of the Islamic state and some of these in higher seats of authority maltreated the Muslims (just because of their hostility to Islam and Muslim.

Metz writes .

In the early period of Islam other troubles and disputes that cropped up between the Muslims and the Christians were due to the maltreatment of Muslims by the copts. One other reason was also that many non-Muslims had amassed so much wealth in a way that the Muslims took it to have been earned by unfair means. (The major portion of their wealth had come from the caliph and the nobles through their misplaced generosity). Under these conditions it is manifest enough that the cause of displeasure was much more of the nature of class strife rather than religious contention.

Islam in fourth Hijri century Vol. I. P. 106

Profesor Arnold wirtes in his book 'Preaching of Islam : The ummayyid caliph, Abdul Malik bin Merwan ahad appointed Ashnas, a Christian citizen of Arha town for teaching and training of his borther Abdul Aziz. When Abdul Aziz became governor of Egypt, he, Ashns accompanied him. And once there taking advantage of his position amassed immense wealth. It is said that he had four thousand slaves and any number of houses and orchards. Silver and gold had little value in his sight. They were carelessly littered everywhere in his house like pebbles. His son collected one dinar from every Egyptian soldier on pay day, when it is known that the Egyptian army was thirty thousand strong. Ashnas lived in Egypt for twenty one years. Imagine the immensity of his wealth.

The Christian medical men too had become plump with the 'fat' collected from the Muslim society. They enjoyed a prestige among the elite of the Muslim community, and Harun Rasheed's personal physician Jibril, in addition to his monthly salary and properties bringing in million dirham annually, used to earn through other sources 0.28 million dinars annually. The other physician (probably an assistant or stand by) too received twenty two thousand dirhams. The highy disproportionate share in the country's wealth had created rancour and envy among Muslims, and they were always looking to a loophole to push their fingers in.

- Preaching of Islam, P. 81-83

An additional reason was also that if the Romans were victorious against the Muslims, the Christians rejoiced openly and this grieved the Muslims and roused evil passions in them against these adversaries - lovingly inspired by their own elite:

Undoubtedly, there have been some Muslim officers of the Islamic state who were strict to the zimmis and took them to task.

But they were rare exceptions. And such officers were greater tyrants to their Muslim brethren than to the alien zimmis. But most of the strict and hard-hearted Muslim officers in spite of their tyranny and excesses in their dealings with Muslims were gentle and equally kind to the zimmis, so much so that the Malikite jurist Allamah Darwir who was the most outstanding among the Ulama of Egypt of his age, writes on one occasion that the officials of his time had given extra ordinary lift to the zimmis in comparison to the Muslims. If only they had put them (Muslims) second in order to the zimmis" The Muslims are often heard saying that if they had only imposed Jizyah on us also like the Jews and Christians and likewise left us alone, free to do what we liked .

- Sharah Sagheer, Marginal Note on Sawi Vol. I. P. 369

Some people without giving serious thought to the Quranic verses and the traditions of the Prophet, unmindful of their real sense and their context, picking up a word from them spread this misunderstanding that Islam is baised against non-Muslims. Particularly the following verses are put forth in which stress has been laid on non-cooperation with the non-Muslims.

For example,

Let not the believers take for friends or helpers unbelievers rather than believers, if any do that, in nothing there will be help from Allah : except by way of pre-condition, that ye may guard youselves from them. But Allah cautions you (to remember) Himself, for the final goal is to Allah.

- Al Quran III: 28

And,

To the hypocrites give the glad tidings that there is for them (but) a grievious Chastisement; to those who take for friends unbelievers rather than believers : Is it honour they seek among them? - all honour is with Allah.

-(Q. IV : 138-139)

And,

O ye who believe : Take not the Jews and the Christians for your friends and protectors : They are protectors to each other. And he amongst you that turns to them (for friendship) is of them. Verily Allah guideth not a people unjust.

(Q. VI. : 51)

And,

O ye who believe : Take not for protectors your fathers and your brothers, if they love infidelity above faith. If any of you do so, they do wrong.

-Al Quran IX : 23

Again,

Thou wilt not find any people who believe in Allah and the Last Day, loving those who resist Allah and His Apostle, even though they were their fathers or their sons or their brothers or their kindred.

- Al Quran LVIII : 22

And,

O ye who believe : Take not my enemies and yours as friends (or protectors) - offering them (your) love, even though they have rejected the truth that has come to you, and have (on the contrary) driven out the Prophet and yourselves (from your homes). (simply) because ye believe in Allah, your Lord : If ye have come out to strive in My Way and to seek My Good - Pleasure (take them not as friends), holding secret converse of Love (and friendship) with them for I know full well all that ye conceal and that ye reveal. And any of you that does this, has strayed from the Straight Path.

- Al Quran LX : 1

Allah only forbids you with regard to those who fight you for (your) faith, and drive you out of your houses and support (others) in driving you out, from turning to them (for friendship and protection). It is such as turn to them (In these circumstances) that do wrong.

- Al Quran LX : 9

To such verses people try to give that meaning that

Islam has preached that we should cut ourselves off from them, hate them and straw our displeasure with regard to them, no matter even if these non-Muslims are close associates and sincere to them in mutual relations. But whoever thinks over these verses, going a little deeper and also cast a glance over the situation in which they were revealed, it will become apparent to him that:

1.   Maintenance of relations has been prohibited only with those who are religiously and ideologically opposed to the believers and not with the neighbours, comparisons and countrymen. Stress has been laid on it that the loyalty of the Muslims in the first palce should be with the Islamic *millet* (community) or the party and not over looking its interests seeking friendship and support in others, (aliens), in preference to those one's own. As an ideological party it is also essential for Muslims since any system or organization, religions or man-made, does not permit any one to have his loyalties transferred to aliens from the kindred.

2.   The friendship and protection seeking which has been prohibited with those who openly demonstrated their opposition to Allah and His Apostle and continually caused hurt to the Muslims, and not with peace-loving non-Muslims as revealed by the following verse;

> Thou wilt not find any people who believe in Allah and the Last Day, loving those who resist Allah and His Apostle.

> - Al Quran LVIII : 22

Apparently enough, opposition to Allah and His Apostle or resisting them does not mean not believing in them, but to fight agaisnt the Divine Message and its preaching, putting up hurdles in its way and causing distress to its subscribers and upholders (preachers) :

---Offering them (your) love, even though they have rejected the Truth that has come to you, and have (on the contrary) Driven out the Prophet and yourselves (from your houses) (simply) because believe ye in Allah, your Lord.

- Al Quran LX : 1

In this verse friendship with the pagans has been prohibited in very clear terms for the reason that the unbelievers had driven out the Apostle of Allah, and the Muslims from their town, Makkah wrongfully :

Allah forbids you not with regard to those who fight you not for (your) faith, nor drive you out of your homes, from dealing kindly and justly with them : For Allah loveth those who are just. Allah only forbids you with regard to those who fight you for (your) faith and drive you out of your homes and support others in diriving you out, from turning to them (for friendship and protection). It is such as turn to them (in these circumstances) that do wrong.

- Al Quran LX : 8-9

Thus the non-Muslims get divided into two compartments: one type comprises those who lived in peace with the Muslims. They neither fought against them nor dirve them out of their homes. To be treated justly and kindly is their right devolves on Muslims.

The other group was that adopted the attitude of enmity and malice towards the believers, they fought against them because of their faith and stood confronting them in every compaign. And it was such people with whom friendship was prohibited - for example the Makkah pagans at whose hands the Muslims had to undergo much suffering.

3.   Islam has permitted the Muslim males to marry girls of the people of the Book. Apparently, conjugal life without love and affection and without mental peace and tranquillity cannot last long. The Quran says :

And among His Signs is this, that He created for you mates from among yourselves, that ye may dwell in tranquillity with them, and he has put love and mercy between your (hearts). Verily in that are Signs for those who reflect.

- Al Quran XXX : 21

That means there is no harm in friendship and love of a Muslim with a non-Muslim. Apparently how can a Muslim help in not loving his wife from the people of the Book, and how can his progeny not run to their grand parents (maternal) for their love and affection from them?

4.   Undoubtedly, Islam places the relationship of faith above all other relationships, whether these others may be on the basis of race, colour or religions. If you were to study Bible you will find great emphasis on that point.

CHAPTER V

THE EVIDENCE OF HISTORY

It is so often witnessed that fine constitutions are formulated and many principle and laws, the choicest that the constitution makers can gather from any source are incorporated in them. But when it comes to practical application, they all lose their significance like beautiful flowers made out of paper—no scent- no beneficence. And those at the helm of affairs overlook them (the commonality) altogether.

But the basic characteristic of the Islamic principles and laws is this that they have a divine origin, and due to this religious stamp on them they are accepted utmost sincerity of heart and enforced in the same spirit. No man-made constitution can boast of this elevated position.

The history of the Islamic *millat* in different periods has been presenting such rare and magnificent examples of tolerance, not witnessed elsewhere.

Some rare and magnanimous incidents of justice and tolerance relating to the period of the rightly guided caliphs have already come for mention in this book. Now let us cast a glance at the history of the Umayyid dynasty and see what picture it presents.

Lowel Durant writes in his book '*Story of civilization*:

· The Christians, Magii, the Jews and Sabian zimmis were enjoying such treatment of tolerance during the

Umayyid dynasty's rule, unparlleled in the history of christendom. They were perfectly free in living up to the dictates of their religion. Their places of worship were safe. They had nothing to do except putting up a particular sign in their dress and according to their means pay one to four dinars annually as tax. This taxation too was limited to combat-fit males. Friars, women, children, slaves, old disabled persons and medicants were exempt. And in return for this tax they were exempted from compulsory military service or defence for the country. Moreover they had not to pay two and a half percent of their annual income as zakat. The government held the responsibility of their protection-life, property and houses. Their evidence was not accepted in the Islamic courts, but they had courts of their own in which their own judges decided their cases according to their own religious laws.

During the Abbasid period known as the golden period of Islamic culture and civilization, making the basic historical sources and the writing of the orientalists, the foundation of his book, 'Islam aur Ahle zimmah', Dr. Kharbotali writes about the condition of zimmis in this regime:

During the Abbasid dynasty there have been many famous person from among the zimmis who rose to fame due to the favours conferred on them by the caliphs. Jarjees bin Bakhtishu was the personal physician to attend on the caliph Abu Jafar Mansur. The caliph had great faith in his medical skill and he enjoyed great honour and prestige at his court. Haroon's personal physician was Jibrail bin Bakhtishu about whom the caliph used to say:.

"Whoever is in need of anything let him approach Jibrail (Gabriel). Whatever he says to me invariably receives approval". The monthly income of this physician was ten thousand dirhams. Another Guebre Masawaih, was also among the favourites of Harun Rasheed, who was paid one thousand dirhams monthly. Moreover, he was paid twenty thousand dirhams annually over and above his usual monthly pay.

Tertone writes : "In stating the merits and excellence of the non-Muslim writers are particularly more generous with their pens. This generosity extended so much that they declared Hunain bin Ishaq as the glory of the physicians of his time and Hibbatullah bin Talmeez they came to call Buqrat and Galen (the most famous almost proverbial early Greek physicians)".

Bakhtishu bin Jibrail (Gabriel) was such a great favourite of the caliph, Mutawakkil, that in his dress and adornment, prosperity and show of wealth, lavish spending and the large number of male and female slaves he tried to come up to the level of the caliph himself. Another Christian Silmavaih, when he fell ill, the Caliph Mutasim sent his son to enquire about his health, and when he died, his funeral was ordered to be brought to the royal palace, and according to the custom of the Christians the funeral prayer was allowed to be said in candle light and incense burning. Mutasim missed a meal that day as mark of intense grief for the departed soul.

Yuhannah (John) bin Masawaih, remained attached to the Abbasid darbar during the regime of several caliphs from Haroon Rasheed to Mutawakkil. He was always present at the royal dining table with the caliphs and the caliphs did not take any meal without him. With Mutawakkil he was so familiar that he often engaged in jokes and exchanged of humour with the caliph.

In the field of learning and literature many zimmis rose to great heights of fame in that period. Tertone writes that in the field of litterature and arts the relations of the Arabs with the subject nations and races were very pleasant based on friendship during the first and the second century of Hijrah. This state of affairs continued in the latter year also. The government used to obtain the services of non-Muslim engineers and other experts in their (building) construction works.

Many zimmis received education from the jurists and other teachers of the Islamic state, Hunain bin Ishaq became the disciple of Khalil bin Ahmad and Sebawaih until he became an authority in the knowledge of Arabic language in his own right.

-Al Mughni, Vol. VIII, p. 136.

Yahya bin Adi bin Hunain was the disciple of Farabi in logic, and in this discipline became the most learned and outstanding logician of his time. Thabit bin Qurrah became the student of a Mutazili erudite, Ali bin Waleed and attained a position in the world of letters. His handwriting was very beautiful. His books furnish proof of his deep insight and depth in knowledge.

- Tabqat-ul-Aulia, Vol. I, p. 185.

Tertone mentioning the tolerance of Abbassids with zimmis writes that Ibrahim bin Hilal can be presented as an example of what height can a zimmi attain in an Islamic state government. Ibrahim had attained such an enviable position that the poets used the logic with him. Izzuddaulah Bawaihi had offered him the important post of a minister. Ibrahim was a staunch followers of his own religion and his relations with the Muslims were very pleasant. He used to correspond with the well known literary persons, Sahib bin Abbad, Sharif Razi and others. It is said that Ibrahim had learnt the Quran by heart.

Muslim authors paid full attention to other religions. Ibn Hazam Undlusi (Spanish) (D. 456 A.H./ 1064 A.D.) had a perfect command over Bible. Ibn Khalladoon had acquired expertise in the knowledge of Bible and Christian organisations. And he has written something about it in his world famous book '*Preface to History*' Qalqirshandi considered it necessary to know about the festivals of the zimmis. Magrizi has made mention of the festivals of the Christians and Jews in great detail, and their different sects, and the great Christian leaders of Alexandria he has mentioned by name.

-Masoodi's book *Al Tanbeeh wal Ashraf.*

Tertone has in conclusion acknowledged that the treatment of Muslim officers with zimmis was much above the demands of the law. The greatest argument in favour of his statement is the construction of a large number of new churches and other places of worship in the purely Arab towns. The offices of the state were never without Jewish and Christian officers. Rather, at times, they were appointed to the highest and most sensitive posts which brought them immense wealth. The Muslims participated in their festivals also (not casually but regularly and their hearts and souls in them).

- Ahle Zimmah fil Islam P. 256

Adam Metz writes :

In the middle ages the Islamic state and the Christian Europe differed manifestly in as much as the followers of other religions lived in the Islamic state in large numbers but not so in the Christian west. The churches and places of worship of other religions were so free as if they were outside the sphere of the influence of the Islamic state. And they had their own rights and laws. The Christians and Jews lived side by side with the Muslims perfectly free in their lives and activities, whereas Europe during this period was totally uninterested in any such concept of toleration.

The famous Egyptian historian Ahmed Ameen writes : in his book 'Zahurl Islam' Part I :

During the Abbasid period since toleration was so common and witnessed every where, apparent even to the casual observer, and the Jews and Christians commanded commercial, literary and martial (relating to war fare) relations and alliances on a large scale. The Christians and Jews were prospering in these states. The unclaimed properties of the Muslims go to the Bait-ul-Mal, but such properties of zimmis were returned to their co-religionists. Similarly, from other aspects too the Muslims furnished full proof of toleration in their dealings with the non-Muslims. As a result of this facility to them the number of Jews and Christians in the Islamic state had become vast enough. In 1185 A.D., in Iraq alone the number of Jews had reached 0.6 million. Such large numbers of Jews had come to reside in Damascus, Allepo, along the rivers Tigris and Euphrates, in Jazirah Ibn Umar, Musal, Hamadan, Asphahan, Shiraz and Samarqand. And the historian Magisi writes that there is a large number of Jews that are citizens of Khorasan.

The tourist Bin Yameen (Benjamin) writes that in 1165 A.D. Qahirah (Cairo) had seven thousand and Alexandria three thousand Jews.

Fifty thousand Christians lived in Baghdad alone. And men from both groups occupied high government posts including those of ministers and governors.

During the latter period, the Uthmani empire too, that extended over vast regions of Asia and Europe presented the same model of toleration.

According to the Uthmani constitution the entire population of the kingdom had similar rights and obligations barring those conditions where modes of worship and religious practices came in the way. The Christians and Jews enjoyed all the political rights which they could ever attain. They took part in all the legal and administrative elections. In the legislative assemblies their rights of representation received full regard. Their representation therein was much greater than their numbers demanded proportionately. At times the allowance touched those limits that their representation was accepted without any legal right to it. For example in the Symerna province the number of Armenians and Jews was so meagre that constitutionally they had no right to elect a representative of their own. But the Turks out of extreme benevolance co-oprated one member of each community for such (special privilege) representation. In most provinces it was the same.

In administrative elections and in provincial councils there was no distinction of majority and minority. And here both the rights of minorities received great regard, and the senior clergy was the members of the district administrative councils. The Uthmani law made no distinction of religion or race in government services. Every one had equal rights with all the rest and any one could get a job in government offices without distinction of Muslims and non-Muslims.

In the eleventh article of the Uthmani constitution we come upon these words :

In the Uthmani empire people subscribing to any religion or *millat* have perfect freedom in their religious acts provided they do not cause breach of public peace, and are not antagonistic and aggressive to the creed and acts of other religions that have been recognized by the state. Right from the establishment of this empire the followers of every religion have enjoyed full freedom. No one was ever given trouble because of his religious creed or acts. Every religious ceremony, of whichever religion it may be, has been performed under the protection of the government. There was no other government in the world in which the subjects belonging to other religions could have enjoyed so much freedom of conscience.

Edmound Inglehart, the French ambassador at Constantinople writes about it :

The privilege and rights enjoyed by the Christian citizens are purely religious and present a marvellous example of religious freedom. All the nations enjoy such vast freedoms and rights in the country's administration that in a way that in their internal and familiar life they have perfect autonomy which no other kingdom has conferred on its subjects. The commission that had visited Constantinople in 1856 to settle terms of the Treaty of Paris., acknowledged during the course of discussions that the rights enjoyed by the subjects in Turkey, were so extra ordinary that any other independent state could hardly tolerate them. In Obe Sleni's words : Turks neither know religious injustices, nor have they any pattern of the Papal Order of the middle ages. As against it their country is a place of safety and peace for the innocent accused persons of the world. Turn the pages of history. In the fifteenth century thousands of Israelites from Spain and Portugal sought asylum in Turkey and have since been passing a life of peace and tranquillity under its protection. In comparison with it even today no Jews can peep out of his window in Athens.

- Turkey aur Tanzeemat

Mr. Philip Marshal Brown is a professor of the Faculty of Law in Princeton University, America writes in his book :

Turkish Law confers all possible right and freedoms on non-Muslims to conduct their internal affairs under the supervision of their clergy. Similarly, the clergy are their administrative officers also in place of the government officials. In other words the clergy are the rulers - independent monarchs. So to say, sort of the state within the state existed in Turkey. This is really worthwhile that Turks in spite of being conquerors very generously conferred their rights on the conquered people, and left them free to govern themselves according to their customs and manners.

This is clear proof of the fact that Turks in the middle ages, when Popes reigned supreme in Europe, under the principle of self-determination conferred on the subject nations the right of self-rule, whereas this right has not been conferred on their subjects by the so-called most civilized nations, championing the cause of so-called freedom.

This freedom has greater significance for the non-Muslim educational institutions. The Uthmani government has entrusted to every bishop the administration of minority schools in its entirety to decide on the issue of syllabus, to recruit teachers and professors for the schools and colleges, to supervise the education and training of the students - all these jobs are the sole responsibility of the bishop. The government does not interfere in any of these matters at all.

The minorities enjoy many financial privileges. For example all the lands belonging to the church are rent-free. The bishop realizes taxes from his community.

Until a Christian has fully paid the fixed amount he can neither be sure of his salvation (denied issue of *letter de cachet* signed by Pope or official permit of entry to heaven at one time sold by hawkers in the streets), nor confess his guilt and sins to the bishop or other clergy for their remission. His children remained without receiving baptism at the Church font (a dip in holy water to mark the entry of a child to regular Christian faith or christening as it is called in religious terminology). He can not get married formally at the church by the minister. And he cannot have a prayer said for his sick. In short the bishops have fixed amounts for all rituals big or small that have a religious tinge and cannot be performed without the intervention of the church. Only the Armenian church makes no demands for money for confession or prayer said for any purpose.

Apart from these taxes there is a national or community tax without paying which a person is thrown out of the community he used to belong to ex-communication. In this way (by extortion) the bishop amasses several millions a year.

Turkey not only provided asylum to the Jews but also the clergy that had been exiled from France like the Jews from Spain. After the division of Poland in 1772, a party there refused to accept subjection by Russia and twenty thousand strong migrated to Turkey. The Sultan welcomed them cheerfully and kindly offered them lands by the river Danube, permitting them self government, according to their own laws, customs and manners. The Cossaks (Russian cultivators) that lived on the banks of river Don, during the regime of Queen Anner of Russia, were exiled for religious reasons from Russia and the Turks gave them asylum near Brussa.

"During the period of world war also the feelings of antagonism did not prevent Turks from kind treatment of the citizens of the Allied countires. In all the western countries the subjects of the enemy countries were extradited, imprisoned or kept under house arrest. Their properties were being confisscated. But the Turkish subjects were allowed to live normally like the days of peace. Rather, many of them came by extra ordinary chances of earning wealth by unfair means particularly in Constantinople and Symarna all those allied citizens having monopoly in tobacco and in the Public Loan office. And the subjects of the allied countries who were in government service and had gone on leave before the commencement of hostilities but could not return due to war, returning only after it was over, full pay for his long term of idleness was paid to them. The Uthmani government maintained the securities and other documents of the banks of the Allied countries and their interests (benefits) were not overlooked. During the war the Ottoman Imperial Bank and Tobacco monopoly were regularly maintained although concerns belonged to the Allied countries. In the western countries even the language of the enemy becomes detestable, so much so that Ezor had changed the name of Saint Petersburgh to Petrograd, since burgh is of German origin. But in Turkey the schools maintained French as a compulsory language during the war even after that Turkey was the only country that, barring the hostile armies and other things associated with them, regarded nothing as inimical.

CHAPTER - VI

COMPARISON

These desirous of a fuller knowledge of the real value of Islamic tolerance ought to study also the treatment meted out to their opponents by the other religious and ideologies during the different periods of history and even today how the staunch believers in modern secular and revolutionary ideologies are treating their ideological opponents in the twentieth century, so much so that they went to the last extremes of tyranny with their own ideological comparisons, treading the same path with them, if they evinced slightest digression.

When the Muslims conquered Spain the attitude adopted them towards the conquered people is worth contrasting with that these so kindly and affectionantely treated, may pampered people, did to them after eight centuries of unparalleled benevolent rule in which period they had made Spain such a beautiful album of learning, light and civilization and culture in which history justly takes pride to this day.

They should also witness that in the modern age which is known as the period of light and civilization in which international organizations like U.N.O. are at work and in which all sorts of tall talk and lofty claims about human rights are so common, how are the Muslims being treated in non-Muslim countries. In Abyssinia where Muslim population preponderates how they are being trampled with impunity, and they are the targets of oppression and tyranny of the worst type. In countries like Russia, Yugoslavia and China where in several regions Muslims dominate what communism did (and is doing) to them. They were not allowed to say their five daily prayers. They were prevented from Hajj pilgrimage. They were deprived of learning their faith and keeping the mosque frequented by the devotees to join congregational prayers. And the Islamic centre of religious activities were locked up by the tyrants (to cut them off from their cherished faith)[17] No justice loving person can justly evaluate the human service with regard to tolerance until he has taken stock made a rather detailed survey of modern secular ideologies and their mode of acting. With them oppression and tyranny, genocide, terrorism and ruination and total destruction are not isolated events but this behaviour with the opponents is a part of their permanent policy. In the way of revolution, Maxists did not only take every sort of tyranny and violence as permitted but regard it essential for revolution, of course with the assertion that aggression has been characteristic of every revolutionary movement. And to make this revolution successful they went on pushing it forward with relevence and wish cruelty constantly. (Anti -revolution phobia keeps them at it).

Dr. Nadeem Baitar writes in his book *"Revolutionary Ideology"* that the philosophy of Marxist revolution rests on this that for revolutionary training

---

17. For greater details and additional information please see Mahmud Shakur's book '*Eritarea* and Habshah' and Shaikh Muhammad Ghazali's book '*Islam Surkh yalghar ke Samne*.'

violence is in itself an essential element. The movement relies on violence for the reason that the common people should be awakened from their deep slumber and activated. And then it may always be rousing them to remain alert and active for their movement, almost constantly shocking and rousing their revolutionary intuition. Violence indicates that revolution be presented before the common people with untiring regularity so that they may not go once again to be overtaken by deep slumber and revolution may never be out of their sight event for a moment. In the words they should not be allowed time to understand that revolution has become a tradition, for that would be the death of revolution.

So before domination over the state generally the nature of violence is individualistic with a view to create an atmosphere of terror and to make the existing authority convulsed, shaky and lottering, so that as the next step control may be taken of the state itself with gradual but perfect sway over it.

Then after effective domination over the state individualistic violence gives way to collective violence which is aimed at strengthening the roots of possession and domination. And for this purpose the annihilation of the opponents - the enemies of revolution is a must, so that the society may harmonise with the new order - the communist Revolution.

The scenes of barbarity, bloodshed and genocide presented by the communists after domination of Russia, crossed every limit. When it was pointed out to them— the comrades of Lenin that if the process continued, three fourths of the pupulation of Russia shall have been annihilated soon enough, their answer was that that had no importance. Importance if any lies in the patent fact that the remaining one fourth may become true and staunch communists.

So during Stalins regime bloodshed was unparallel in the history of the world. Many of its ghastly episodes surfaced during the time of Khruch chev.

- Khruschev's speech in the 20th Conference of the Communist party.

The interesting fact is that the revolutionaries to prove justification of barbarity meted out to the opponents refer to the old history of revolutionary religious, particularly Christianity in the middle ages. They say that Tolstoy and Hitler took their clue from the Christians. Undoubtedly, Christianity preaches peace and love and in its early period of pitiful helplessness it remained the target of many tyrants (both the Jews and pagans of that period). But no sooner had it come into authority and rule (or aid and support of Pagan Rome which imposed its own terms on them and Christianity had to pay dearly for this support and strength from outside, it accepted a pagan hue at the intervention of their masters) it left no record of tyranny and oppression unbroken and scored its own (higher records) also mere mention of which makes the listener's hair stand or end.

When the philosophy and ideas of Ibn Rushd began to spread, particularly among the Jews, and their popularity was on the increase day by day, the fury of the

Spanish Church burst upon the Jews and the Muslims alike. It ordained whole sale expulsion of Jews from the country in such a way that they could take with them articles of daily use and other goods of a paltry nature, but no gold and silver were they allowed to take away with them. The Jews made all possible haste to leave the country to save their lives, but so many lost theirs due to hardships of starvation and the labour involved in journey and other hazards - running away for dear life.

In this way in 1052 A.H. the Church ordered the Muslims to leave Isabella by a route which does not lead to any country (outside Spain) or they would be massacred, meaning thereby that in case of their refusal to embrace Christianity they would be slain either way. This fury reached a pitch where even the Christians who differed from the official Christian view became the target of their ire.

These who have studied the history of Christianity must be knowing very well that in 1325 A.D. in the well-known session at Nicea what treatment was meted out to Areos, a learned Christian pro from Egypt. He was not a believer in the divinity of Christ. So they sitting in session after expelling all the members at variance with the official creed issued a verdict. Areos should be hanged, his books should be burnt and their possession and reading should be declared a serious crime. His supporters should not only be expelled from services but exiled also. And after that whoever is found with a book by Areos or he is found to be a supporter of him should be hanged. So as a result of this oppression and tyranny those believing in the unity of Allah left the scene and became untraceable. The difference of opinion Christians on some principles of Gospels and their exegeosis and interpretation for example whether the holy ghost is a part of both the father and the son or only that of the latter, bread and wine form part of the body or not, whether Christ had both the natures divine and human or not, etc. became the cause of severe violence which cost hundreds and thousands of lives, and one group in the other in great trouble and disress.

When the Protestant cult came into existence through the hard struggle of Martin Luther, Catholic Church pressed its full force into action against it and there was much blood shed. The Paris massacre became most notorious when on 24th August, 1572, the catholics invited Protestans to come together and try to reduce their differences of opinion to a minimum. When the Protestants had come in the darkness of the night the host fell on the sleeping guests like wild carnivorous beasts. Next morning's sun witnessed that the roads of Paris were ruddy with the Protestant's blood. Pope himself congratulated Charles IX on this "magnificent achievement". And the catholic kings and leaders landed this Satanic act of fratricide very highly. And when the Protestants got the upper hand and they repeated the same gory episode with the catholics exhibiting the same barbarity and beastliness. Luther said to his followers and supporters that whoever of you can do something openly or secretly should not pail in making short shrift of the catholics.

- Maseehiyat by Dr. Ahmad Shibli P. 51-52

Inqilab-e-Nazariyat by Dr. Nadeem Baitar
P. 710

So there should be nothing to wonder that these religious wars of Europe took a very disgusting form. It is said that in Germany alone in these interveine religious wars the majority of German nation was annihilated and most of the busy towns, pull of bustle and activity became mounds of ashes.

As for the crusades even the barbaric movements like Nazism and communism of the twentieth century are reduced to a poor show in comparison with the beastliness demonstrated there in. During these wars the Christians themselves, who regarded some of their brethren misguided, made them the target of awful oppressions and tyrannies. They did not flinch even from ploughing the fields littered with the enemies corpses, and converting them into the fertilizers of the earth. Even the so called good religious leader: were ever ready to add fuel to give. The military men, the so called heartless soldiers in spite of their hard-heartedness were at times moved to pity, the distressed and oppressed. But these religious leaders regarded mercy and moderation rebellion against religion, and were day and night tirelessly busy in shaping a Christian world which could accomodate only Christians. They were not at all prepared to give any other any right whatsoever - not even the right to live. So the aliens were either forced to get converted to Christianity under the sword or mercilessly put to death. The Christians started missionary activities to propagate their religion at a much later stage. (for a long enough time it was Christianity or sword).

The procedueres of inquisitions even today are enough to make the hair stand an end. From 1481 to 1808 A.D. these inquisitions punished 0.34 million people. Out of them 0.2 millions were burnt on the pyre. (Some were mercilessly broken on the rock). Brifault writes in his book "Islam and Christianity along with Science and Culture". According to the historian's estimate in Europe during the period of its propagation, 7 to 15 million were killed from Christendom. In those days Europe's population was much smaller than it is today. England's catholic queen Marie had it once announced that since the souls of infidels will ever be burning in hell so in imitation of the divine retribution in the life Hereafter, there can be nothing, better than burning them here also".

The well known Egyptian author, Syed Qutub of late lamented memory, writes in one of his papers, "Are the Muslims prejudiced?"

This is an open and gloring fact that in the history of mankind only the Muslim dominated regions where tolerance was the order of the day, and the minorities have been dealt with on the basis of purely humanitarian spirit and sentiment. The Islamic societies guaranted their modes of worship, religious creeds., business and work (labour), in short all sorts of freedoms which the non-Muslims societies even today in the different parts of the world have been denying to those of a different creed, race and colour.

But in spite of all the toleration and kind heartmen to the aliens, the Muslims are accused of prejudice, whereas even in this twentieth century the non-Muslims throughout the world are metting out to Muslims the treatment which is not witnessed anywhere in the world where the Muslims are in power and authority.

In fact the allegation of prejudice agaisnt Muslims and propaganda of intolerance against them is a part of that campaign carried out to demigrate Islam and Muslims and to create feelings of hatred in the world opinion against them in an extremely organized and planned manner.

From Indonesia and Malaysia to Afghanistan and Iran and from Turkey to Egypt and Sudan, in all the Muslim countries the minorities have been living in peace and tranquillity for centuries. In other countires so much attention is never paid to the condition of the minorities. The Muslim countries are not even acquainted with the name of the detestable communal prejudices. Not just today but throughout the history of Islam this situation has persisted, particularly, in the period when the Islamic Shariah was in force there, unparalleled justice has prevailed.

In the history of mankind the Islamic world alone has been providing the followers of different creeds opportunities of benefiting by all the rights and sureties. It is Islam alone that makes its followers responsible for the freedom, creed and modes of worship of others. The Quran permitting the Muslims to fight for the freedom of creed, say :

Did not Allah check one set of people by means of another, there would surely have been pulled down monasteries, churches, synagogues and mosques in which the name of Allah is commemorated in abundant measure.

- Al Quran XXIII : 40

Is it not a fact that Quran mentions the mosque after the places of worship of other people ?

But the Muslims are prejudiced in spite of all that:

Here we shall take stock of those with tall claims of freedom, progressiveness and tolerance in different parts of the world how savagely they are treating their Muslim minority. And on the other side how are the minorities in the Muslim countries living in perfect peace and tranquillity.

Let us take you to Russia to start with where it had been making loud propaganda of the equality of man, freedom, progressiveness and enlightenment throughout the world. We shall show you that the savagery of oppression and tyranny that were perpetrated on Muslims, its mere mention makes the head of humanity bow down with shame.

During the last four centuries the Czars kingdom was regarding the worst enemy of Islam and Muslims. Giving the prejudice of Christianity represented by the cross and crusades a disgusting colour was making life for Muslims unbearable. With the aid and support of the government Christian missionaries and the offical machinery did everything, to oppress Muslims, they could. But compared with the endeavours of Communist Russia to eradicate Islam and Muslims and their annihilation by whole sale, the painful history of anti-Muslim compaign of terrorism of the Czarist regime pales into insignificance.

Here we shall quote an example from the magnificent book on history by Yusuf Wali Shah and Alkiri. *"The Tragedy of the Muslim Community in Soviet Russia,"* in which the most dreadful and painful situation of "Muslims in Russia has been portrayed most vividly.

In the beginning of the 16th century A.D., the bishop of Qazan, Herr Haman, wrote a letter full of reproach to Czar, Theodore, saying in the most in-flammatory and instigating style how due to failure of the Christian missionaries the return of most converts to their old faith, Islam and their devotional acts in the mosques which they had rebuilt (after demolition by whole sale). Prompted by this report of the bishop,the Czar took very storm steps against the Muslims. They were deprived of their properties and were compelled to live in a particular locality of Qazan which has been specifically built for them. A Russian noble was made their ameer (leader or commander). Moreover, Muslim youngmen were compelled to marry Russian girls and women (of advanced age) and the defaulter was to be jailed. And once their hands and feet tied they were mercilessly flogged and hurt in other ways. But it appears this much of painful chastisement was not considered enough to cool down their brutal passion of revenge. So he ordered that centuries old mosques be demolished and the Muslims driven out of their homes and towns.

"But the Balsheviks kept their secret plans very skilfully under cover and about their stand regarding the faith they were secretive until authority and rule got transferred to their hands and their feet were firmly established a solid ground. When they became satisfied from the world outside (that it was now with them) they (the communist party) started sending well-organized military bands to various parts of the country. These agnostic bands adopted every possible measure of wiping out clean all traces of the faith, and Qazis and Muftis (issuing religious verdicts), school teachers, preachers, imams (leading the congregational prayers) and Muazzins (criers to prayer) and the ulama were killed in large numbers. The schools, mosques and other religious centres were forcibly snatched and occupied also with still greater force. In Quran and other Muslim areas the courts running other the Islamic Shariah and the centres of Islamic verdicts were declared illegal and closed. Later, the mosques and schools of religious learning were converted into stables godowns and cinema halls etc. Which no civilized law anywhere in the world permits. And they did not stop at that. Collecting all the available copies of the Quran and other religious books they made a bonfire of them. Even in the most barbaric early periods of humanity we do not come upon such a degradation of morality. Only the mosques of a very high architectural value and beauty combined were spared, to be preserved to delude the world outside by showing them as the time-honoured monuments of Russia.

Qaram and other Muslim regions of Russia longed so eagearly to the soul-stirring sound of Azan, (call for prayer), since no one dared perform the devotional act for fear of life itself. (Azan or cry of the Muazzin is the sign of life of faith and piety for Muslims).

The compaign of anti-religious movement had reached its climax in 1938. This was the period when after burning the copies of the Holy Quran and other religious books, conversion of mosques and religious schools into communist institutions and putting to death the ulama and other elite of the religious hier archy or deporting them to the Siberian cold hell, all traces of faith had apparently been erased. In 1938, one night when the last group of ulama was arrested in Zului and after various kinds of torture they were taken to the water works of Fuad Canal on the shores of Black Sea. Then in the stillness of the night they were taken in separate vehicles to the slaughter houses of communist's paradise. The attendants who participated under compulsion in this ignoble, disgusting and despitable act are even now doing existence in Turkey and European countries as refugees and can bear witness to it.

This horrible incident, sending a tremoring body is nothing compared with the tortures and anguish caused to the innocent Muslims in Turkistan where 44 million of them had been living after its conquest and rule over it. It has now after the genocide compaign and well thought out and organised plans, been reduced to 26 million. Western Turkistan is under the hedgemony of Russia and its eastern portion under the ascandency of claims.

Isa Yusuf Alaptegin[18] has mentioned in his book 'Muslims behind the curtain' many methods of torture some of which are such as a civilized mind cannot have even a concept of them. Hence we are mentioning only the less disreputable and shameful ones:

1. Nails were driven into their heads until they reached the brain (causing death).

2. After sprinkling petrol on their (the prisoners') bodies they were set on fire.

3. The prisoners were made to stand in a line and their armed guards made them easy targets.

4. The prisoners were closed in dark cells without access of air and were kept closer there until starvation and suffocation made short shrift of them.

5. Putting iron helmets on their heads, they were connected to the electrical mains.

6. The head of the prisoner was tied to one end and the body to another machine and both started in the opposite direction at the same time. This game continued until the prisoner died.

7. Every part of the body was branded with red hot iron rods.

8. Boiling oil was poured over the bodies of the accused.

---

18. Isa Yusuf Alaptagin was a citizen of Turkestan, and had written this book after making his escape good from the Russian hell overcoming in surmountable difficulties.

9. Iron nails and sharp pins were introduced into the bodies of the prisoners.

10. Iron nails were driven into their finger nails.

11. The prisoner was securely tied to a four poster bed and left to die of starvation and thirst.

12. During the biting cold of winter season the prisoners with naked bodies were made to sleep on sheets of ice. (A true copy of the cold hell of Siberia - brought home).

13. The hair of the head were uprooted in such a way that even the skin of the scalp came off with them.

14. Iron combs were vigorously passed over the bodies of the prisoners.

15. The prisoner's bodies were secured with ropes and then burning material was cast into their mouths and noses.

16. The hands of the prisoner were tied behind his back and then a heavy stone was put on his back.

17. Binding his hands with ropes he was hung up from the roof and remained dangling the whole night.

18. They were beaten with sticks to which pointed nails had been fixed.

19. With sword and (butcher's) knife the body was chopped into bits.

20. Holes were bored into the bodies of the prisoners, and then a knotted rope was passed through the hole and drawn forward and backward like a saw. This was repeated so that wounds may not be allowed to heal.

21. To make the prisoners stand on their feet for a long time, their ears being nailed to a wall.

22. They were thrown into ice cold water of pools in mid-winter.

23. The fingers and toes were tied to gather firmly.

24. Women were stripped and then beaten mercilessly. And such shameful and disgusting crimes were perpetrated on them in this state which human modesty does not permit mention of.

In view of the above mentioned facts look at the claims of the communists who made mention of the article 124 of the Russian Constitution with loud applause, though Stalin had changed it in 1936. In the said article it has been said : "For the freedom of the creeds of all the citizens it is declared that in Soviet Union religion shall be independent of the government. All the citizens shall be free to perform religious rites or call people to agnosticism."

But the fact is that to teach very young children agnosticism the government had made all sorts of arrangements. Where religious education is concerned to make its position explicit it will be sufficient to mention the following law of the Russian Penal Code:

"In government schools or a private school, those arranging religious instruction can be sentenced to one year's vigorous imprisonment."

And during the term of this incarceration all those measures of torture were adopted which have come for mention earlier.

The Muslims have been the victims of brutal punishments, and tortures in China that are disgraceful to humanity. And the way they have been annihilated through genocide and massacres on a large scale are unparalleled.

As a result of organised efforts to annihilate Muslims in Russia, according to the communist party's mouth piece 'Pravada's confession,, in some parts of the country 40% of the Muslim population has been put to an end. The communists did not repeat the story of Qaram in other cities except in Muslim areas. So they had selected Muslim community only for all their barbaric genocidal activities. And this was regarded reasonable in Russia.

The Muslims of Qaram town were so much affected by the savagery of Russians that they had come to nurse feelings of intense hatred and malice against the communists. So in the second world war when the German armies entered Russia the Muslims were led to think that the extreme hostility existing between the Germans and the Russians may prove a blessing to them. But they had forgotten that the same spirit of crusade against Muslims is common to Russia and Germany. The Europeans can be inimical to one another and can get divided into several hostile groups also. But where the question of Muslims comes in they present a united inimical front to these aliens' - the Muslims. So after the entry of the Germans into Qaram town the dreadful situation the Muslim faced at the hands of German soldiers can be much better appreciated as related by Yusuf Wali Shah and Akiri :

"Then it will not be possible to say that the Muslims suffered at the hands of the Russians because of their enmity to and contempt for Russian communism. For not withstanding the anti-Russian feelings of German armies they paid the Muslims for opposition to communism in a way that Russian brutality of the worst type pated into insignificance.

Thousands of Muslims who had surrounded at great risk to themselves, only to get detached from the Red army, were taken hundred of kilometrers from the war front, bare headed, bare footed and naked, being driven like sheep. They were refused food and water on the way and clothes to cover their nakedness. On the way if a victim due to exhaustion lagged behind, he was shot even without a question. A word of protest from any one was fatal, the fate of laggards awaited them round the corner.[19]

Muslim prisoners were sorted out from the entire lot of prisoners of war, for this beastly treatment. These Muslims prisoners wanted only this much from Germans that their independence should be acknowledged in principle and they should be left alone so that they may organize their army to fight against the Russian communists and drive them away without the help of Germans, with Russian arms alone. The Muslim leaders

---

19. *"The Tragedy of Muslim Qazan in Russia."*

negotiating with misgivings about them or it may fear any foul play with the German army at the rear, they (Germans) may retain their hold over those centres so that it may be satisfied with the good intentions of those who want to strike against the communist forces. But Germany rejeced this offer of Muslims saying that Germany will get the better of and take over Russia with pure German blood alone.

In Abyssinia and Ethiopia the Muslim population is not less then 55%. In some areas it is even 65% the rest of the 35% is divided among the Christians, the Jews and the pagan idolators. These statistics are also according to the Italian census of 1936 and the facts and figures are those printed by the foreign consulates. Whereas the Muslims have been largely overlooked and under-estimated in every field. There is evey likekihood that the Muslim population may be more than 65%. But in their Christian state how the Muslims are being treated, an idea of it can be had by the following most moving facts :

1.   After the end of Italian Imperialism the Abyssinian government confiscating two thirds of the Muslim properties handed them over to the Christians. Morevoer the impoverish Muslims further heavy taxes were levied on them.

2.   The government provided all sorts of facilities to the Christian missonaries, whereas the Muslims were not even permitted to move from one place to another to preach to their Muslim brethren elsewhere. The Christian missonaries expressed hope in their reports that due to

poverty and ignorance of Muslims and the absence of men rousing them to and teaching faith, they will be able to have the entire Muslim population converted to Christianity within five years at the most.

But as Allah's Grace and bounty would have it, their wishful thinking and pious hopes to naught, and their plans were ruined.

3.   In Abyssinia attention to religious institutions was given to Kafa, Jaisame and Lalodhra provinces by the Muslims. In Jaisma alone there were more than sixty schools for childrens' education. But its annexation to Abnyssinia was declared and mischeviously its Sultan Amir Abdullah Bin Sultan Mahmood bin Daood was incarcerated. At this stage the government took hold of these schools. Most of them were closed. The syllabus of the rest was changed in such a way that there was no trace left of Arabic language and Islam in it.

4.   The government of Abyssinia did all it could according to the available means to spread education among the Christians. About two hundred primary and secondary schools were opened in which the Muslim students were not more than three percent. And even they were those Muslim students who had to be admitted due to the compelling cause. In spite of Muslim majority not more than 5% of the allotment of the Budget for education was spent on their education. Moreover, the government schools were kept totally aloof from any influence of the Arabic language and Islam.

5.   In the above mentioned areas when the

Muslims moved the ministry of education that in the schools of this particular region education of Islam and Arabic languages be arranged, in some schools, teachers assigned for Islamic education were appointed who were not at all competent for this job. Moreover, no particular period was allotted for such education. Rather the teachers concerned were directed to acquaint the students with elementary knowledge of Islam, the five times of prayer, number of units or rakats and the obligatory elements of the devotional acts in the recess or interval in the time schedule of the school. But during the interval these teachers did not get time to teach the students even these elementaries and the entire educational session every year passsed without doing anything.

6.   In 1951, according to the report of an Egyptian delegation touring Abyssinia the government selected students having completed the college courses, for foreign education so that when they return highly qualified, may take over charge of high government offices. Among them were two Muslim students also, selected on grounds of high percentage of marks. They had made all the preparations for moving out of the country, but when it came to actually starting on their journey for unknown reason they were not allowed to proceed.

7.   There were seven major educational institutions belogning to Muslims based on religious instruction and Arabic language. They were run with the aid   and support of subscription and generous contributions of Muslims. About three thousand students

were benefitted by these institutions. In spite of difficulties and obstacles they continued functioning unitl
1949. The government according to their programme
wanted to eliminate Arabic language and religious
instruction from these schools, but the administrative
committees refused to oblige. After that the government
adopted such an attitude towards these administrative
bodies that the members found themselves helpless. And
in this way Islamic education and Arabic language were
excluded from the syllabus.

8.   A certain school requested the ministry of
education that some Egyptian teachers living in Abyssinia,
should be allowed to teach their students some
disciplines on non-working days. But the ministry refused
to oblige.

9.   An embargo was put on the entry of Arabic
books in Abyssinia and their study was banned. The Arabic
journals and newspapers were allowed entry after minute
scrutiny.

This is not a tale of darkages but painful facts of
the twentieth century. About sixty five percent citizens
of Abyssinia are being made the target of all sorts of
injustics causing great distress and applications, just
because they subscirbe to Islam (the most detestable
name on the hit-list of Christianity and Judaism besides
pagan idolators throughout the world).

And that is not the only tale of woe of Muslims.
In Abyssinia Muslims are kept far from government
services, they are barred from military service for fear

of creating a martial sentiment in them. But in spite of all that :

Muslims are a prejudiced Community :

In Yugoslavia the lives of two million Muslims are in great peril, particularly those of German Muslims whose lands were usurped by Yugoslavia in the second world war with the help of Russia, Britain, France and America.

Here it will not be out of place to mention that Americans and Englishmen during the trial of strength with Axis powers armed the communist elements in Germany so that they may start their guerrilla war fare activities against the Axis powers. But for this very campaign they did not supply the Muslims any arms. Why? Since the blood of Crusaders was circulating in their bodies. And with all their animosity against the communists, when it came to the arming of one of the two groups, communists or Muslims they opted for their kindred, the communists (in preference to "aliens" and "deadly enemies"). (Whatever is happening in Yugoslavia, genocide of Muslims and the gloating over it of the entire Christian word is not secret - Total purge of Christian Europe).

America, Britain and France are the most blatant claim- ants and standard bearers of progress, freedom, civilization and humanity and their concept of a "Free World", to them depends on that group of imperialists who, over looking the demands of the times throughout the world is at war with the principles of freedom and humanity.

These champions of freedom scored on unparalleled record in perpetrating ignoble and disgusting crimes against the lovers of freedom throughout the world from Tunis to Algiers and Morocco and from India and Kenya to Vietnam. Probably by the term "Free World" they mean that they must have a free hand to massacre of freedom and independence, no holds barred.

The "free world" has been perpetrating such crimes which send a tremor through one's body. And all this was done to strengthen the foundations of western culture in the "Dark continents". If the people inhabiting these parts of the world were not prepared to become civilized at the hands of their vangwards", the missionaries, swords, guns, bombers and tanks did the job. Could there be any quicker medium of taking the light of civilization to the backward nations of the world?

And it was this "free world" which has driven away the nations from their lands of birth as it was done in Palestine, although later on refugee funds were raised and founded on a permanent basis, for this distressed and displaced person and tents were pitched in the deserts to accommodate them, since that was also a principle of the "free world" to make a show of kindness and sympathy for the homelees wretches.

To purchase newspapers, writers, parties, organizations and men and women is also amount the basic principles of the "Free World", since the civilization of the barbaric coloured races of the world with guns and tanks is an operation taking very little time, for dressing polishing and making them easily tractable for the "Free World" (in their satanic operations), only such weaponry (saleable media men, hypocritic leaders of parties and organizations and men and women with no conscience and sense of honour and with ever-changing faces and veils) can be of use in a perpetual war of nerves.

In this freedom of the "Free World" not that in keeping with the Jungle law (Might is Right), where there is no one to stop the ravenous beasts from free use of their, sharp claws and ferocious fangs?

France is called the Father of Freedom. (The Britishers have their own claims to democracy and freedom). But did not the Franch like a group of savage robbers put the political leaders to death in their colonies through fraud, treachery and other guiles. And as a face-saving device before a watchful world opinion did they not resort to the absurd logic that it was an internal, affair of France and no one in the world had any right to interfere. In 1830 after taking possession of Algiers, France had been perpetrating the most heinous and disgustingly shameful crimes agianst the innocent Algerians. And in this worst demonstration of savegary and beastliness it had the full support of Britain and America.

It is France and it alone that led the crusading armies of European powers nine hundred years hence. And the French armies proved the most savage and ferocious and ravenous beasts in the face of most human treatment of the Muslims having due regard for "Morality of Warface" taught to them by their faith.

And it was France that in the episode of Suez Canal played a foul and most treacherous game and left no strategem untried in taking possession of it - unsurpation becoming only a whiteman. It was due to this fraudulent behaviour that Egyptian armies had to face defeat in the Nile Delta region at the hands of the Britishers.

The French delegate in the Security Council supporting the Britishers made extremely shameful attacks on Egypt and taking leave of all civilized manners and a civil tangle he heaped the most foul abuse (on a peaceful country they wanted to rob it of its major source of national income). (But then France, considered to be the most cultured among the European nation, has its own norms of utilitarian morality or immorality and "no one has any right to interfere in its internal afairs" coloured savages the least).

And again it was France that made the teaching of Islamic disciplines and Arabic language a penal offence, and treated the defaulters in this behalf like thieves and robbers quenching its thirst of Muslim blood with that of thousands of innocent Algerians.

I have myself witnessed in America that a crowd of whites in a frenzy fell on a black American citizen on a public road, and laid him flat with kicks. The police remained a silent spectator. In such incident of chastisements and torture of the blacks and even lynching, the police becomes active only when the crime (according to the plan) has been completed and the crowd has dispersed like wild beasts.

This is the real face of the champions of "Freedom and Equality". Freedom and Equality indeed.